D1589290

Towards Europe

The Story of a Reluctant Norway

P.I.E. Peter Lang

Bruxelles · Bern · Berlin · New York · Oxford · Wien

Paal J. Frisvold

Towards Europe
The Story of a Reluctant Norway

Europe of Cultures
Living Stories
Vol. 16

Cover picture: Aud Gloppen.

The book was subject to a double blind refereeing process.
No part of this book may be reproduced in any form, by print, photocopy, micro-film or any other means, without prior written permission from the publisher. All rights reserved.

© P.I.E. PETER LANG s.a.
Éditions scientifiques internationales
Brussels, 2018
1 avenue Maurice, B-1050 Brussels, Belgique
www.peterlang.com; brussels@peterlang.com

Printed in Germany

ISSN 2031-3519
ISBN 978-2-8076-0372-1
ePDF 978-2-8076-0373-8
ePub 978-2-8076-0374-5
Mobi 978-2-8076-0375-2
DOI 10.3726/b13198
D/2018/5678/17

CIP available from the British Library and from the Library of Congress, USA.
Bibliographic information published by die Deutsche Nationalbibliothek Die Deutsche Natio-nalbibliothek lists this publication in the Deutsche Nationalbibliografie; detailed bibliographic data is available on the Internet at ‹ http://dnb.d-nb.de ›.

To Dad

Initiative belongs to the little people – for their lives are in jeopardy.
Bjørnstjerne Bjørnson

Preface

The broad-based transatlantic collaboration of the post-war period which brought stability and prosperity to Europe and large parts of the world in general, is currently under pressure. US President Donald Trump's politics and leadership style are shaking our established views and threatening trade-policy cooperation based on ground rules common to all the countries concerned. Britain's warned-of withdrawal from the EU (Brexit), the final outcome and consequences of which are still discernible, is a shot across the bow for Europe's 60-year-long integration process. Political developments in other central EU countries are also cause for concern. In other words, we are living in very exciting and uncertain times.

There can be no doubt that the institutions of the OECD, the WTO and the EU, together with cooperation on security policy in NATO, paved the way for extensive, rule-based collaboration based on collective rules and mutual obligations, which also contributed to economic growth in Europe and internationally. These organizations have knitted our communities together by opening up markets and by giving economic agents stability and predictability. They have not resolved all the market economy's ongoing problems by any means, but they have established common arenas founded on mutual respect for one another based on the realization that all countries stand stronger together than alone.

Unemployment, the influx of refugees and weak economic growth mean that populations are turning their anger on foreigners and competition from other countries. Few appreciate that inequality and poverty stem primarily from poor wealth distribution policies, lack of access to education and lifelong learning, and underdeveloped welfare schemes. Mutual economic dependence between countries has led to a need for more wide-ranging legal, binding international cooperation. Economic policy based purely and simply on the needs of the nation-state with no consideration for international relations has proved to be increasingly unsatisfactory, indeed even harmful. Thus, the populist anti-EU lobby has found a "whipping boy". In this context, there is a growing need to remind the man and woman in the street why and how we have arrived where we are today. How did the European integration process come about and, for Norway's part, what gradually convinced us to become part of it?

During my career as a civil servant and ambassador in the Norwegian diplomatic service, I have had the privileged position of taking part in the development of the post-war collaborative fora. As part of Norway's negotiating delegation with the EU on participation in the EEA from 1989 to 1992 and Norwegian membership of the EU from 1992 to 1994, I have seen first-hand how challenging it is to reach agreement between countries. It also gave me an understanding of the intentions underlying the EEA Agreement, as compared with the expectations we had. It was chiefly a matter of avoiding Norway being left out of the ever closer economic cooperation that was developing in Europe. As Norwegian Ambassador to the EU and President of the EFTA Surveillance Authority (ESA), I was involved in shaping the early, and perhaps the most important, years of the agreement.

Much has been written about Norway's relationship with the EU, the EEA and ESA. This book is not an academic discourse on these aspects. The book provides the reader with a personal account of the way the author sees that relationship working, viewed from Paal Frisvold's position as an employee at the EFTA secretariat and later as a representative of Norwegian organizations and the business community in Brussels.

The book "Towards Europe" gives a broad and pithy picture of Norway's approach to European integration right from 1905 to the present. One of the interesting things about the book is that it challenges the established perception that the Norwegian people's resistance to the EU stems from its time as a union with Denmark and Sweden. Instead, Frisvold highlights an outdated self-portrait of being "a poor country on the periphery of Europe", with industry and particularly farming vulnerable to international competition. Today that situation has been turned around. Norway has one of the world's strongest economies, and technological progress, including communications, has made its distance from the continent far less significant than previously. Conversely, a protectionist approach to its food, fish and farming has helped cement old and outdated attitudes towards the outside world. As Frisvold alludes to, there are currently some 20,000 people in jobs in Germany, Denmark, the Netherlands and Poland whose livelihood is made from processing Norwegian farmed fish. For the fact is that the EU tariffs increase with the degree of processing in Norway. These are jobs that could have been allowed to exist along the Norwegian coast if only we had been able to sell processed fish to the EU countries duty-free.

In "Towards Europe", Frisvold also produces valuable information about the way the day-to-day relationship between Norway and the EU is handled within the framework of the EEA Agreement. Here he highlights several concrete examples and stories that I myself was involved in, illustrating Norway's exposed and challenging political position when our interests run counter to rules and regulations the EU countries have already spent years negotiating and adopting. Few others have managed to show how this intricate negotiating game is played out in practice, and how the importance of the matter for the individual country, not the size of the country, is crucial to the result in most instances. That makes the book an important source in the debate on the EEA, whether for Norway or for any other countries that might be considering a similar system of agreements. Not even the comprehensive report *Utenfor og innenfor* (NOU, 2012: 2) managed to reproduce the actual and complicated negotiating conditions on the EEA Committee as Frisvold does in this book. Here the book also shows how Norway's political room for manoeuvre is growing ever narrower, in line with the EU's own political and economic integration. Now as ever, there is a difference between sitting around the table as a full member and sitting up in the gallery during negotiations when one's own interests are at stake.

In the last part of the book Frisvold examines the EU's challenges and plans to solve four main areas by 2030. He questions whether Norway's present association can be satisfactory for such a well-resourced and open economy as Norway's, dependent as it is on close and mutually obligating collaboration with the outside world. Here the book focuses on many of the areas challenged by President Trump's change in policy and the Brexit negotiations, continuing to make the book topical and relevant for a long time to come. This is the setting for the debate on the significance of international cooperation and the EU for society and individuals alike.

These days there are few people who believe in Norwegian membership of the EU. A need has therefore arisen to defend Norway's existing affiliation, so that the EEA Agreement does not go up in smoke as well. During the Brexit negotiations, and in the light of populist calls to leave the EU, the book will make an important addition to an open, thorough and unbiased debate on the weak and strong points of the EEA model. The book contributes to that in a simple, insightful and sometimes humorous manner. It should be read by everyone who is interested in European integration and how the EEA model functions in practice.

Einar Bull

Ambassador of Norway to the EU (1996-2001)

President of the EFTA Surveillance Authority (2002-2006)

31 January 2017

Foreword

Two quotations made me write this book: one from Knut Frydenlund's book *Lille land, hva nå?* (1982), the other from Haakon Lie's memoires entitled *Skjebneår 1945-1950* (1985). Frydenlund's book says that "In an international context Norway could occasionally crawl under the table, but we could not take up permanent residence there". Haakon Lie is referring to Willy Brandt's colleague, "who knew every word of foreign origin except one-solidarity." Almost every one of us has surely encountered a similar opinion of Norway when in contact with friends on the continent we belong to.

Both statements are descriptive in many ways of Norway's role in modern-day Europe. At the same time, they are rather out of kilter with the depiction of history many people have grown up with. This book gives a different version of the story of Norway's relationship with the world at large.

The official Norwegian Europe review *Utenfor og innenfor* ["Outside and Inside"], in which an expert committee assesses Norway's relationship and agreements with the EU, provided a copious and detailed description of the area covered by the EEA Agreement, and its huge importance for Norway. Little space is devoted to the political interaction between the EU and Norway, however. Here, I wish to provide an insight into the practical everyday life of the EEA Agreement and show how the relationship between the EU and Norway works.

Finally, the book looks ahead and examines the main features of the key European initiatives in store for us. I should like to thank the publishers Origami forlag for having given me this opportunity. In particular editor Wegard Kyoo Bergli for his indefatigable positivity and guidance. Thanks also to Anne Karin Sæther, Ingrid Kylstad and Anne Berg, who inspired me to pen the manuscript, as well as for comments and input from Alf Ole Ask, Caroline Klæth Eriksen, Erland Frisvold, Jón Baldvin Hannibalsson, Dag Wernø Holter, Sten Inge Jørgensen, Bjørn Olav Knutsen, Finn Langeland, Lars Erik Nordgaard,

Hans Jacob Orning, Torun Reinhammar, Georg Riekeles, Steinar Solheim, Aage Stangeland, Sylo Takaru, Kåre Verpe, Guttorm Vik and Kjetil Wiedswang.

I would like to thank Laurence Pagacz at Peter Lang for agreeing to publishing this book as well as precious help from Sarah Rooman.

I also wish to thank my wife Martine and our daughters Zoë and Ruby for their patience in living with a writer.

Paal J. Frisvold

Brussels, December 2017

Contents

Prologue

European Policy From Heaven

In 1870 a hot-air balloon from the heart of Europe came crashing down in the mountains of Telemark. The crash provided the prelude to widespread popular support for France's war against Prussia, one of Norway's first and last popular engagements in European politics.

The people quickly flocked to the square outside the Château de la Muette on the outskirts of Paris one grey November evening in 1870. Few had seen the revolutionary new means of conveyance first-hand: a hot-air balloon laden with people and supplies. None of the many thousands who turned out could have envisaged in their wildest imagination that the expedition they were witnessing would end up on Mount Lifjell, near Bø in Telemark – far fewer still that it would usher in widespread popular involvement in a Great European conflict.[1]

With Otto von Bismarck at the head, Prussia had surrounded Paris after having overpowered Napoleon III's army in Sedan. The tactics now involved were to starve the Parisians into total submission and surrender. After several months of a full blockade around the whole of Paris, winter was imminent, and signs of desperation began to appear. The Parisians had a wealth of ideas for breaking the German blockade: everything from sending women with Prussic acid in their thimbles to kill German soldiers to releasing the wild animals in the zoo and letting them loose on the enemy.

President Louis Jules Trochu wanted to order the Minister of the Interior, Léon Gambetta, and his soldiers, who were besieged in Tours outside Paris, to join forces with the troops in Normandy. There they were to conquer the city of Rouen, then penetrate Bismarck's troops at their weakest point: from the north. The President's problem was to

---

[1] This entire story and the details have been taken from Einar Østvedt's book, *Den første luftferd over Norge*, Oluf Rasmussens Forlag, Skien, Norway, 1968.

communicate the plan of attack to the Minister of the Interior in Tours, as no one on the ground was able to get there owing to the German blockade. The solution would turn out to be a hot-air balloon with two men carrying the President's secret message sewn into their uniforms.

By 10 p.m. on 24 November the hydrogen-filled hot-air balloon, La Ville d'Orléans, was ready to depart from the large, open square at Château de la Muette, a castle on the outskirts of Paris. It was the same castle that would host the negotiations on the fate of Europe after the Second World War up to the present day. The open basket, or gondola, conveyed Captain Paul Rolier and his co-pilot Deschamps skywards and over German troops. The basket was full of thousands of letters, food, wine and water, and large sandbags were used to adjust their height and speed.

After just a few minutes and a good hundred metres up in the air, the balloonists were surprised by bullets flying past on either side. They had been spotted! In their panic, they began ejecting the sandbags in order to climb higher and beyond the reach of the German bullets. It was only when the altimeter showed 2,700 metres that they stopped ejecting.

"Neither of the balloonists driven northwards from Paris at breakneck speed in the Ville d'Orléans that pitch-black November night had any inkling that they had now embarked on one of the most dramatic balloon voyages in history", writes Telemark's great local historian Einar Østvedt in his book *Den første luftferd over Norge [*"*The First Air Crossing over Norway*"*]*. For hours on end the French President's envoys had to sit in that little gondola, frozen stiff and staring at the sky, at the clouds and anything that might provide a clue about the landscape beneath them. As the sun's rays peeked out one morning, Rolier first saw a carpet of green forest. He would later realize that his eyes were deceiving him and that they were just above the sea. Dreading landing in the ice-cold waters, the two men threw out more sandbags and allowed themselves to be blown further out of control. Nineteen hours and 130 nautical miles further north, both their clothes, hair and beards were stiff with ice. Trees and forests were exchanged for white plains and mountains. Rolier judged that it was "now or never", and together the two of them managed to leap out of the gondola basket and down into the deep snow. The two Frenchmen walked all night long outdoors, and only the following morning – when they were famished and freezing cold – did they find a sledge track, which led them to a small timber shack. They knocked, but no one opened, whereupon they entered, sat down by the meagre embers of the wood-burning stove and flung themselves upon some paltry dregs of coffee and left-over potatoes. A short while later, two brothers stood in the doorway: Loggers Harald and Klas Strand stood face to face with the French balloonists in the little timber shack without any of them understanding a single word of one another's language. Using sign and finger language, they arrived at France, Paris, Norway and Telemark. They had dropped down onto Lifjell in Telemark, 800 metres above sea level. They were 200 kilometres from Christiania, as Oslo was called then, which they had to get to as rapidly as possible in order to have the message from the President in Paris sent to the Minister of the Interior in Tours.

The sensational balloon voyage would attract great attention all over Norway. The following telegram from P. Nielsen, a district sheriff in Krødsherad, to the bailiff in Buskerud spread like wildfire across the whole country – like a sensation in a country isolated and starved of news from foreign parts: "This afternoon a hot-air balloon from Paris came down in Krødsherad. There were a number of sealed mail bags, six live doves, but no people." National and local newspapers got hold of the news. Both *Morgenbladet* and *Aftenbladet* wrote about the story, and the wildest speculations and rumours were printed in papers around the country.

Long before the French balloonists reached Christiania, the news of their arrival caused a great stir. Crowds of people swarmed together at Vestbane Station, where the train was due to arrive, and outside the French Consulate's office in Karl Johan's Street, where the throng shouted "Vive la France!".

Telegrams and greetings poured in from the whole country, from Tromsø in the north to Hamar, Tønsberg and Mandal. In Christiania receptions and gala performances were held, with circus and theatre, all in honour of the Frenchmen. The biggest celebration was mounted in Gamle Logen, the old Freemasons' Lodge on Count Wedel's Square, where an independent organizing committee had invited 800 guests, with a further 100 outside. After Headmaster Gjertsen expressed the Norwegian people's affection for France in fluent French, the Norwegian Students' Choral Society struck up Jonas Lie's ode "To France". Close to one percent of the entire population of Christiania (at that time 100,000 inhabitants) had turned out. In a society devoid of radio, TV – not to mention the Internet and social media – mustering one percent of the capital's population commands some respect.

Norwegian, Danish, Swedish and French flags adorned the facade of the heavy grey edifice housing the Masonic Lodge in Christiania. Songs, speeches, applause and champagne corks went off in perfect unison, and the evening's keynote speaker, Mr Bjørnstjerne Bjørnson, took to the stage and delivered a fiery address in honour of the French guests: "Just as this hot-air balloon that was sent up by the enthusiasm of the French fatherland, by France's peril and valour, came drifting here towards us in a whistling storm, so too from France have risen, out of the great earth, mostly in the hour of need, great thoughts, ideas of redemption, travelling out on the wings of the storm across the world and careering towards our mountain, only to fall back to earth." Bjørnson's speech also played on the parallel with Norwegian society: "For more than half a century we have had France to thank for some of the greatest notions we have lived off. In this moment, too, when France itself seems to be a balloon drifting in foul weather, it is a shining example to the rest of us, particularly us ordinary folk. For it shows what a people without an army can do when it wants to. It is without precedent in world history!" The applause was interminable, and after Rolier's speech of thanks the two balloonists were carried shoulder-high in triumph around the great hall several times.

The first balloon voyage over Norway generated great enthusiasm, even amongst most Norwegians. On the trip from Lifjell in Telemark to present-day Oslo, it caused a ripple of curiosity and sympathy that developed into a powerful feeling of solidarity with France. Money collections were held across the land. In Hamar alone they collected 630 francs, and from Kopervik on the Isle of Karmøy came 100 francs. As he was about to depart from the quayside in Christiania on the English steamship SS North Star on 1 December, bound for England, the French consul was able to hand over a cheque for the staggering amount of 23,800 French francs – an amount equivalent to 1.32 million Norwegian kroner in today's money.

While the Norwegian government had to consider its position on the Swedish government's sympathy and commercial relations with the Germans, the Norwegian people's attitude had taken a different direction. Two Frenchmen's incredible journey to the north ignited people's heartfelt desire to show sympathy and support for resolving Europe's conflicts.

PART 1

NORWAY IN EUROPE
RESISTANCE AND GOOD FORTUNE

CHAPTER 1

The Post Hoc Country

"Does Norway belong to Western Europe?"
Château de la Muette, Paris, 17 September 1948

The elegant British Chancellor of the Exchequer, Hugh Dalton, stubbed out his cigarette in the ashtray recessed into the conference table and blew out the smoke, which settled like a carpet of fog in the square between the negotiating tables. He raised his voice and turned his gaze firmly towards his Norwegian colleague: "Does Norway belong to Western Europe?"[1]

The Head of the Central Bank of Norway and former Second World War resistance fighter, Gunnar Jahn, sank down into the leather chair as he cast a worried look over at his Swedish colleague in hope of support. This was strong meat coming from Norway's closest ally during the war. Jahn realized that the Norwegian negotiating strategy had failed.

Hall C in the historic Château de la Muette on the outskirts of Paris was full of fifty or so smartly dressed gentlemen – finance ministers from seventeen countries, helpfully assisted by other high-ranking officials, advisers and ambassadors. Jahn was Norway's chief negotiator in one of the post-war period's most important conferences: on the reconstruction of Europe. Allies and enemies were seated closely in order to make room for everyone around the conference table. Together they discussed how Europe should proceed in order to reconstruct the war-ravaged continent. The scene was unique in its own right. Countries which had hitherto been at war with one another at regular intervals over the past thousand years were seated around one and the same table.

---

[1]   N.A. Røhne, "De første skritt inn i Europa", *Forsvarsstudier*, 5/1989, p. 13.

Jahn now considered that there was more than meets the eye to the political realities in Europe as they looked from home. The basic premiss behind the Norwegian attitude was – and had long been – that Norway could play a bridge-building role between east and west. The government had invested a great deal in maintaining that rapprochement but was now met with little understanding during the Paris negotiations. Instead, their attitude came across as provocative and raised doubt as to the Norwegians' loyalty and intentions towards their closest wartime allies: those who had contributed so much to liberate us from the German occupying force. Jahn reported home to the government that Norway had no choice but to abandon its objective of being able to accept millions of badly needed American dollars *without* entering into closer economic cooperation with her neighbouring European countries.

The aid granted by the Marshall Plan was to have huge significance for the recovery of the Norwegian economy after the war. So where did the Norwegian government's hostile attitude towards the Americans' generous assistance come from? The answer is complex, of course. The fact that Norway was a poor country on the periphery of Europe with just 40 years' independence is one possible factor. The desire to keep out of the countless conflicts between the continent's superpowers at any cost is another. Or was the hostile attitude due to a naive belief that a small country can be instrumental in solving the world's problems by standing alone?

Norwegian reactions to European cooperation projects before and after the Marshall Aid attest to a Norway that was reluctant: not just about the framework for the largest aid programme by far up to that point in history, but also to practically all initiatives for binding cooperation with other countries.

Løvland's neutrality line and Norway's first foreign policy

Following the dissolution of the union from Sweden in 1905, Norwegian foreign policy hinged on guaranteeing Norwegian neutrality. Norway had to pursue a policy of non-alignment. The country had an open economy and depended on being able to trade with as many countries as possible. Norway's geographical location, remote from the European continent, was in itself viewed as protection.[2] It gave the country a chance to remain outside of the continent's game of power politics.[3] That is a distance Norway wished to retain.

Such was the strategy for Jørgen Løvland, the first Norwegian Minister of Foreign Affairs. During the great North Sea Conference of 1908 all the countries bordering on the North Sea assembled in Paris to establish agreement and respect for all nations' coastal limits – all except Norway. And the government achieved its objective: Norway was not even mentioned in the North Sea Treaty. Norway was a non-country, a spectator rather than a participant.[4] Thus began Norway's independent foreign policy.

The strategy of neutrality lasted all the way through the first part of the First World War; then her neutrality was challenged at sea. The war came quite unexpectedly to Norway, which had no clear foreign policy, but one of the world's largest shipping fleets of all.[5] The idea that foreign-policy events might have consequences for the Norwegian economy was alien to the government. Half its merchant fleet was lost. Nine hundred vessels were torpedoed and 2,000 seamen lost their lives. Recent research shows that as many as 14,000 to 16,000 Norwegians took part in the war on the side of other countries.[6] During the First World War, Bergen was what Casablanca was in Hollywood's version of the other: a refuge where enemies and allies could trade, remain in transit and prepare for perilous passages across the North Sea. This was also a time when Norwegian shipowners were making big money from the risky journey across the water to Great Britain. The British were regarded as the Norwegians' protectors. That was one of the reasons why Norway had elected the Danish Prince Carl king: because he was married to Maud, daughter of the British king, Edward VII, a fact which Prime Minister Gunnar

---

2   R. Tamnes and K. Einar Eriksen, "Norge og Nato under den kalde krigen", in *Nato 50 år. Norsk sikkerhetspolitikk med Nato gjennom 50 år*, Norwegian Atlantic Committee (DNAK), p. 1.

3   *Ibid.*

4   R. Berg, "Norges utenrikspolitisk historie fra 1905 til 1920", Rogaland College Centre, No. 8/1994.

5   W. Keilhaug, *Norge og verdenskrigen*, Oslo: Aschehoug, 1927, p. 85.

6   N. Brandal, O. Teige and E. Brazier, "Kvinnelige pionérer ved fronten", in the newspaper *Aftenposten*, 2014, 11 September.

Knudsen made no bones about: "We shall place our trust in the British nation, mindful of the new link forged by our Queen!"[7] After Germany deployed full-scale submarine warfare in 1917, Norway switched to being a "neutral ally" in favour of the Entente Powers of Great Britain, France and Russia.[8] It was the first indication that Norway could no longer isolate itself from Europe's conflicts.

Nonetheless, the experience from the latter part of the First World War did not change Norway's line in foreign policy. Norway still wished to pursue its non-aligned role and support the universal amalgamation of all the world's nations. Norway's mission, therefore, was to make sure the countries of the world did not ally and regroup any differently. Norway had to prevent group formations.[9] The strategy was followed up by Prime Minister and Minister of Foreign Affairs Johan L. Mowinckel's foreign-policy line during the interwar period. This was the prelude to a deeply rooted belief, in both Norwegian political circles and the diplomatic service, that Norway would be able to play a bridge-building role in the conflicted world that lay before us.

Pan-Europe and the idea of a United States of Europe

The government's neutrality line was not shared by everyone. Fridtjof Nansen spoke out in favour of close European cooperation, a kind of "United States of Europe". A group of Europe-friendly MPs from the Norwegian Parliament (*Storting*) called "The Committee of Interested Parties in Oslo" raised this idea with the Prime Minister, Ivar Lykke, in 1926. They wished to place the idea of a united Europe on the political agenda and asked for the Prime Minister's view of a joint Scandinavian plan to set up a United States of Europe. The Prime Minister replied that the very idea of entering into any form of cooperation between the

---

[7] R. Berg, Norsk utenrikspolitikks historie, Vol. 2, Norge på egen hånd, 1905-1920, Oslo: Universitetsforlaget, 1995, p. 96.

[8] R. Tamnes and K. Einar Eriksen, "Norge og Nato *under den kalde krigen*", in *Nato 50 år. Norsk sikkerhetspolitikk med Nato gjennom 50 år*, Norwegian Atlantic Committee (DNAK), p. 1.

[9] N. Røhne, "Norwegian attitude towards the Briand Plan", p. 12, Professor Frede Cappelen's comments, Castberg's comments on Briand's memorandum, *Norwegian Ministry of Foreign Affairs' archives*, 4/26 J. No. 08505, 1930.

Scandinavian countries would be an impediment to broader European cooperation. "Norway's priority was to strengthen the League of Nations", Lykke wrote.[10]

In 1923 the 28-year-old Austrian Richard Nikolaus Coudenhove-Kalergi published the book *Pan-Europe.* Coudenhove-Kalergi was preoccupied with the national self-assertiveness that dominated European politics. In 1927, he organized the first congress of the Pan-European Union, attended by Albert Einstein, Thomas Mann and Sigmund Freud, amongst others. In the 1920s the Austrian's foremost opponent at the League of Nations in talks on European cooperation was Norway's delegate, Christian L. Lange. He was the father of Halvard Lange, later to become Minister of Foreign Affairs in Einar Gerhardsen's government and a towering figure in the history of Norwegian foreign policy. At that time, Christian L. Lange was one of the most respected Norwegians in international politics. In 1906, he was appointed first secretary of the Parliamentary Committee on the Nobel Peace Prize, a prize he himself would later be awarded together with the Swedish Prime Minister Hjalmar Branting for their work on the Inter-Parliamentary Union. Lange was a keen supporter of Norwegian neutrality policy from 1905. In the mid-1920s Lange was asked by the League of Nations to accompany Coudenhove-Kalergi on his tour of the USA to repudiate and undermine the idea of the Pan-European Union. The League of Nations regarded the vision of Coudenhove-Kalergi as a threat because a united Europe would weaken the global position which the League of Nations wished to achieve.[11]

The Briand Plan and the first Norwegian debate on Europe

In 1929 the French Minister of Foreign Affairs, Aristide Briand, tabled a motion before the League of Nations to establish a European Union. Briand's proposal was a continuation of the work on the Locarno Treaties, which provided for a reduction in German debt

---

[10] N. Røhne, "Norwegian Attitudes towards the Briand Plan", p. 5.
[11] N. Røhne, "Norwegian Attitudes Towards the Briand Plan", *IFS Info*, No. 8, 1991, Oslo.

and the demilitarization of Germany's industrial heartland, the Ruhr District, in the Rhineland. For this, the initiators of the agreement, the US and UK foreign ministers, Charles Dawes and Austen Chamberlain, received the Nobel Peace Prize in 1925. Between them, the countries of Germany, France and Belgium would subsequently reach agreement on their post-war national borders, and peace seemed assured in Europe. This work was also considered worthy of the Nobel Peace Prize, which was awarded to the German and French foreign ministers, Gustav Stresemann and Aristide Briand, in 1926.

The Locarno Agreements were regarded as the beginning of an entirely new epoch in European history. Fridtjof Nansen delivered the speech on behalf of the Nobel Committee on 10 December 1926, when both prizes were awarded. In the Nobel address, Nansen said, amongst other things: "so closes a chapter in [European] history".

Aristide Briand's proposal to establish a European Union was launched during the League of Nations' session in 1929, first in a meeting devoted to the European delegates, then in plenary. But during the Paris discussions in autumn 1929, the Norwegian Prime Minister and Minister of Foreign Affairs, Johan Mowinckel, failed to turn up to listen to Briand's presentation to the European delegates. During the presentation of Briand's Plan to the League of Nations' plenary meeting, Mowinckel sat quiet as a mouse. Nor did Mowinckel utter one word about Briand's initiative during his address to the plenary on behalf of Norway.

One of the reasons for Mowinckel ignoring Briand's project was a suggestion from the Norwegian Ministry of Foreign Affairs' adviser Frede Castberg and former Nobel Peace prize winner Christian L. Lange. Neither of them showed any support for European cooperation of this type. Castberg thought a united Europe would provoke the Soviet Union and distance the USA. His attitude reflected the previous Minister of Foreign Affairs, Løvland's, watchword of non-alignment and Norway having to prevent the formation of power blocs. Lange pointed out that a political organization could not be expanded just on the basis of geographical location, and highlighted the dissolution of the union between Norway and Sweden in 1905 as an example of failed forms of supranational cooperation.[12]

---

[12]   N. Røhne, "Norwegian Attitudes towards the Briand Plan", p. 11.

Minister of Foreign Affairs and Prime Minister Mowinckel wished to give conflicts a wide berth and maintain the freedom to provide all parties with shipping services. In this way, he joined the ranks of Norwegians sceptical about the European integration initiatives during the interwar period, concentrating instead on perpetuating Norway's neutral line.

The *Storting* received Briand's motion in 1930 and for the first time had to adopt a position on the idea of European cooperation.[13] Briand wanted to set up his own European institutions, with a permanent secretariat and a political council. The aim was to develop close political dialogue to lay the foundation for a European federation. Briand proposed an independent European market with the free flow of capital, goods, services and people, virtually identical to Jacques Delors' initiative 50 years later. In the *Storting* the proposal was met with scepticism and did not generate any broad-based political debate. In fact, no representatives took up the cudgels for European cooperation during the autumn session of 1930. The initiative put forward by Briand and the reception it was accorded at the League of Nations did not even get a mention.[14] The rumours about Briand's proposal for a United States of Europe flourished in the press. The leading article in *Arbeiderbladet* (as the daily newspaper *Dagsavisen* was called from 1923 to 1997) made fun of the fact that it was just as dire as the French King Henry IV's initiative 300 years earlier.[15]

Thus ended the only Norwegian public debate on Europe during the interwar period. The paradoxical thing is that the Nobel Committee's decision to reward European peace work two years in a row did not fuel any serious debate on the same topic in government or among popularly elected members of the Storting.

"This was the first dawning of the day after the long darkness", Nansen said in his speech to the Nobel Prize winners in 1926. The contrast with the government's and the Storting's attitude is striking.

---

[13] N. Røhne gives a detailed and interesting description of the Briand Plan and the reaction it was met with in Norway, as well as the treatment it received at the hands of the Norwegian government and parliament. "Norwegian Attitudes Towards the Briand Plan", *Norwegian Institute for Defence Studies*, No. 8, 1991.

[14] Norwegian parliamentary proceedings, 1939, 7b, pp. 1550-1568.

[15] *Arbeiderbladet*, 18 July 1929.

Nothing ever came of the Briand Plan, and the League of Nations proved quite powerless after Germany withdrew in 1933 and Adolf Hitler was preparing the run-up to the Second World War. Bit by bit Hitler's Germany invaded parts of Europe. First Austria in March 1938, then the Sudetenland in September of the same year. At that time, no one was willing to risk forfeiting peace by standing up to Hitler. On 30 September 1938 Hitler and Great Britain's Prime Minister, Neville Chamberlain, signed a German-British peace treaty. Chamberlain returned from Berlin jubilant. Six months later Hitler broke the agreement and invaded the rest of Czechoslovakia. Now Hitler really was deemed untrustworthy. When Hitler invaded Poland on 1 September 1939, France and Great Britain declared war on Germany.

Even in the face of patent German aggression in Europe, Norway insisted on maintaining her neutrality. So outstanding was the government's faith in its neutrality line that it consciously pared down the Norwegian armed forces to a skeleton defence known as "neutrality protection".

Against mobilization. The German invasion of Norway

Despite French and British proposals to mine the Norwegian coast, the Norwegian neutrality line remained strong right up to that fatal morning of 9 April 1940. Then the Norwegian notion of non-alignment and neutrality took a hefty shot across the bows. Even after the Dutch naval attaché Bert Sas and the Norwegian-wed George F. Kennan from the US Embassy in Berlin both sent detailed descriptions of the naval rearmament going on in North Germany and the battleship Blücher's departure for Oslo, the government stuck to its guns on its neutrality position. No mobilization, no cry for help.

My uncle, Paal Frisvold, the chief of staff's personal adjutant at the Minister of Defence's office at the time, described the *Storting's* and the government's inability to act in his private memoirs from the war. Rasmus Hatledal, his superior and chief of the Norwegian defence's general staff, had suggested mobilizing the army's field divisions to the general staff and the Minister of Defence, Birger Ljungberg. When his frustration overflowed, despite his fervent loyalty to the hierarchy, he complained to his adjutant about the lack of military and political dynamism: "I have no support, from either the Commanding General or the Minister of Defence." On the evening of 8 April Colonel Hatledal rang adjutant Frisvold from the *Storting*, where the strained situation had been discussed. No decision was taken other than to have a new meeting the following morning. On the eve of 9 April, after the air-raid alarm had sounded and the German battleship Blücher sailed up Oslo Fjord and approached its fatal destiny near the fortress of Oscarsborg, Frisvold was woken by the phone and asked to report to the Chief of General Staff's office immediately. Having arrived safely at the ante-room, he overheard his superior, Colonel Hatledal, in conversation with government cabinet ministers Trygve Lie and Birger Ljungberg. That was when Hatledal cried: "But Ljungberg, silent mobilization means that every single man has to have written orders, and there's no time for that." Whereupon Trygve Lie butted in and said: "It's time to go and get a bite to eat now, Ljungberg," and with that they rushed through adjutant Frisvold's office and vanished.[16] Just hours before the Blücher was torpedoed at the narrowest strait in the Oslo Fjord, Norway's ministers of defence and trade agreed to send out a letter drafting Norwegian soldiers into service. The government did not want to deviate from the neutrality line for fear of doing something that might provoke Hitler's Germany. It was not even willing to announce full mobilization of Norwegian troops when the Germans were literally inside Norway's borders.

The episode is illustrative of the government's lack of willingness and ability to take decisions. The government had neither insight nor understanding of the events taking place. The episode illustrates how deeply rooted the neutrality policy must have been among the Norwegian civil service and the political milieu. Norway's foreign-policy leadership prior to the Second World War has been discussed extensively in the history books of the post-war period. Viewed in the light of the Norwegian attitude towards European cooperation, one might ask whether it was based on a lack of understanding of what was afoot beyond the country's borders. Was our diplomatic service not able to pick up on and verbalize the consequences of developments on the continent? Or was there a lack of ability to question the deeply anchored belief that Norway was a poor, remote country primarily concerned with keeping our distance from countries that might lead us into conflicts?

---

[16] P. Frisvold, "Litt om det jeg var med på i de fem krigsårene", *Aftenposten*, 1984.

"Europe is not an entity"

The neutrality line pursued by Norway since the dissolution of the union in 1905 would not change materially after the shock of the Germans' invasion on 9 April and the outbreak of another world war in Europe. Certainly, the German invasion did force Norway to adopt a stark position on the side of the Western powers, and the government did enter into a defence alliance with Great Britain in 1942. Conversely, the Norwegian Ministry of Foreign Affairs' attitude towards European cooperation proved to be dominated still by the body of ideas from 1905. Norway's attitude would emphasize "supporting the universal union of all the world's nations and preventing bloc formations".[17] Responding to an enquiry by the British Foreign Office in the summer of 1942 about the interest in new and binding cooperation on the European continent the day Nazi Germany would be defeated, the Norwegian government in London replied with a point-blank refusal: "We doubt the expediency of using the term 'Europe' in serious political deliberations. Europe is not an entity."[18]

The government's reaction was identical to the wording used by Carl Joachim Hambro, President of the *Storting* and a right-wing politician, in his book the year after. That corroborates the consensual thinking on foreign policy among Norwegian political parties and was in tune with the attitude towards Hambro's political opponent Trygve Lie. In the book *Crossroads of Conflict. European Peoples and Problems*[19] from 1943, Hambro goes as far as to deny the existence of any European problem, reasoning that "Europe does not exist and never has existed".[20] In the book he goes on to claim that cooperation between European countries is just as unnatural as cooperation between California and Japan "owing to language, race and tradition". Only two years previously, on 7 December 1941, Japan had gone to war with the USA with its attack on Pearl Harbor.

---

[17]   O. Riste in J.J. Holst (ed.), *Norwegian Foreign Policy in the 1980s*, Oslo: Norwegian University Press, 1985, p. 14.

[18]   AAO, Frihagens archive, Box 5 "Hovedlinjer i norsk utenrikspolitikk".

[19]   C.J. Hambro, *Crossroads of Conflict, European Peoples and Problems*, New York: The Church Peace Union, 1943, p. 3.

[20]   *Ibid.*, p. 4.

Hambro's view of European cooperation contrasted starkly with his Austrian colleague Coudenhove-Kalergi and his ideas about establishing a United States of Europe. The Austrian carried on Briand's initiative and had ideas that would later inspire the Frenchman Jean Monnet, President of the Coal and Steel Union after the war, who talked of "building union among people not cooperation between states".[21]

When peace came on 8 May 1945, the government hesitated again. Norway was uncomfortable about having to appear as an ally of the USA and the other Western European countries. That attitude came to the fore right after the war when the government received an enquiry from the superpowers, asking whether Norway, together with eight other countries, might take on secretariat-related tasks for the Paris Peace Conference in 1946. This was a purely practical voluntary job, with no direct financial gain. The invitation was turned down. The government felt that such a clerical task might place Norway in situations where the government was forced to choose between the dawning alliances in Eastern and Western Europe.[22]

Churchill and the Norwegian iron curtain – a Norwegian vision of a non-aligned world

Norway's fear of showing solidarity with the Britons and Americans by becoming party to the dawning Cold War was deep-rooted. Early in 1946 King Haakon had personally invited Winston Churchill to come to Norway to receive the accolade and thanks he deserved after his efforts during the war. Churchill was to be hailed a prominent leader of the allies and acclaimed for the close friendship he had shown Norway, the king and the government. Just after the invitation had been sent on 5 March 1946, Churchill held a historic speech to the American people in Fulton, Missouri. In the same style and form as the famous speeches that kept up morale and motivation during the war, Churchill described the "iron curtain" that was in the process of splitting Europe asunder:

---

[21] G. Mak, "Europa. En reise gjennom det 20", *århundret, Cappelen Damm*, 2008, p. 564.

[22] H.Ø. Pharo, "Bridgebuilding and reconstruction. Norway faces the Marshall Plan", *Scandinavian Journal of History*, May 1 (1-4), 1976, pp. 125-153.

the frontier with the Soviet Union's sphere stretched from Stettin in the Baltic to Trieste in the Adriatic. The speech lay the foundation for the understanding that a Cold War had taken root between Eastern and Western Europe, and that the world had to prepare itself for rivalry between East and West. Churchill played on the Americans' dread of Europe turning to Communism and falling into Stalin's hands.

The speech did not go down well with the Norwegian government. It put into words the trend towards a break-up of Europe and the need to choose between two blocs. The irritation at Churchill's description of political developments was so strong that the Gerhardsen government chose to call off the visit. The Norwegian Ministry of Foreign Affairs was instructed to inform the man who had led Great Britain and the allies to victory and been instrumental in saving the world from Hitler's tyranny that he was no longer welcome in Norway. There was no one at the Ministry of Foreign Affairs able to voice the sentiment in words. Instead, the Ministry sent an enquiry to their British colleagues at the Foreign Office: could they not tell Churchill "on the quiet"? The request was rejected out of hand. Finally, King Haakon himself had to write Churchill a letter explaining that the visit had to be postponed indefinitely. Churchill replied: "I shall wait until the situation one day gets better. Or much worse."[23]

It would be two years before Churchill finally came to Norway and was given the reception he deserved. By then the Soviet-controlled Communists had staged a coup d'état in Czechoslovakia, the Soviet Union had strong-armed Finland into accepting "neutrality", and the Berlin Blockade was just days away. The Norwegian vision of a non-aligned world lay in ruins, and Churchill was at long last welcome.

---

[23]   H. Lie, *Skjebneår 1945-1950*, Oslo: Tiden, 1985, p. 176.

CHAPTER 2

Château de la Muette

After the Second World War, international cooperation was in its tender infancy. European cooperation was on the drawing board, and a number of initiatives and proposals were put forward. Most, however, were ill-suited to the old Norwegian approach towards European integration and mutually binding cooperation.

Before the outbreak of the Second World War, Norway was a poor country. Five years of German occupation and a war-torn economy had not helped matters. The occupying force had printed off money in the Bank of Norway, contributing to high inflation and money of little value. During the course of the war, price levels rose by more than 50 percent.[1]

Clothes, shoes and food were difficult to get hold of. There was a great dearth of essential raw materials like coal, oil and steel to build up the industry and infrastructure needed to get the country's economy on its feet. These were products and raw materials Norway did not have itself but had to buy with hard currency, which in practice meant American dollars back then. Textile rationing continued until 1954, and the regulation of house-building and car sales lasted right up till 1960.[2]

The château in the 16ᵗʰ arrondissement of Paris, Château de la Muette, was the headquarters for the negotiations on the Marshall Plan aid, officially referred to as the European Recovery Programme. It was not the first time the idyllic château in the French capital was the subject of historic events. Prior to the French Revolution in 1789 the château had been Louis XVI and Marie Antoinette's romantic haunt. After insurgents had left the place in ruins, it underwent costly

---

[1] Norwegian Central Bureau of Statistics (now: Statistics Norway) (SSB), Norges økonomi etter krigen, Oslo, 1965. https://www.ssb.no/a/histstat/sos/sos_012.pdf, pp. 313-314, diagram 58 on p. 318 and diagram 59 on p. 323.

[2] See http://www.arkivverket.no/manedens/sept2002/rasjonering.html.

reconstruction by the Rothschild family. During the Second World War the German occupation force used the château as an operations centre for the German Naval Command. In the summer of 1944 American marines took over the château after the invasion of the Normandy coast and the liberation of Paris.[3]

Thirteen billion dollars was to be divided between Western Europe's 16 war-ruined countries, equivalent to 210 billion dollars in today's money.[4] A massive 5 percent of the USA's total gross national product would give Western Europe a gigantic springboard to get it out of the economic crisis caused by the war.

Allies and enemies squeezed in around the conference table to make room for everyone. Together with the Americans they discussed how Europe should proceed to reconstruct society. The scene per se was unique, for these were the countries that had been waging war with one another at regular intervals over the last thousand years. The war-ravaged continent where nearly 50 million people had died so senselessly was sorely in need of access to capital and goods in order to rebuild the countries. The Americans stepped up, but required coordinated economic cooperation – something a number of countries had difficulty agreeing to.

The tense situation with a Cold War dawning only helped complicate the Norwegian attitude towards the Marshall Aid. The recipient countries were pegged to the US economy because the money they received had to be used to import American goods. The heroic image of the USA from the liberation of Europe was both reinforced and prolonged by linking Europe to the American economy and exports. In many European countries, the Communists had played a key role in the Resistance Movement and the liberation from German occupation, and were therefore in a strong position politically. These countries had both economic and ideological arguments for opposing the offer of help from the Americans. A market economy was not what Europe needed, they felt.

3   OECD. History of Château de la Muette. See http://www.oecd.org/general/
     historyofthechateaudelamuetteoecdheadquartersparis.htm.
4   S. Brandslet, "Planen som endret Europa", *Aftenbladet*, 2007. See http://www.
     aftenbladet.no/nyheter/lokalt/article460643.ece#.U7Ki_Y2SxnY.

The opposition to a US-dominated market economy made itself particularly felt from the Norwegian government. It became clear from the instructions issued by the government in Oslo to the negotiators around the crowded conference table at Château de la Muette: the government did not wish Norway to take part in supranational cooperation that might weaken Norwegian sovereignty and its ability to protect Norwegian industry and jobs. Demands to liberalize trade would mean that Norway could no longer maintain protective schemes in the form of high customs duties such as the Norwegian planned economy was based on before the war. The government feared that the country's economy would be outcompeted by Swedish and Danish industry and agriculture. Opening up Norwegian markets would cramp its scope for self-regulating with an eye to distributing society's benefits fairly and thus widen the wealth gaps in society. The view that Norway had a small and fragile economy that required protecting from Denmark and Sweden was taken as read. Sweden had developed a strong and robust economy during the war. Only by means of customs barriers could Norway rebuild its economy and develop its own competitive national industries, it was argued.

The other main objection to accepting the Marshall Aid was Norway's resistance to entering into any cooperation that tied the country politically to a Western bloc formation and diluted Norway's desired role as a bridge-builder between the superpowers.[5] This problem was amplified when, early in 1948, the Soviet Union rejected the Americans' offer of the Marshall Aid and instructed its allies in Central and Eastern Europe and Finland to do likewise.

At one point the government even maintained that it had no wish for a plan for the reconstruction of Europe, but rather a body to evaluate the need for credit and access to greenbacks.[6] This was possibly inspired by Sweden's national patriarch, Tage Erlander, who stated: "We need no financial support. What is paramount is to ensure that dollar-poor purchasing countries can pay for our deliveries in

---

[5] R. Tamnes and K.E. Eriksen, "Norge og Nato under den kalde krigen", in *Nato 50 år. Norsk sikkerhetspolitikk med Nato gjennom 50 år*, Norwegian Atlantic Committee (DNAK).

[6] H.Ø. Pharo, "Bridgebuilding and reconstruction. Norway faces the Marshall Plan", *Scandinavian Journal of History*, May 1 (1-4), 1976, pp. 125-153.

dollars."[7] The Norwegian government argued that the Marshall Aid Secretariat in Paris should not be made permanent. Norway could just accept an interim organization. Last, but not least, cooperation between the Scandinavian countries must *not* give the impression that a Scandinavian bloc was being formed. The Soviet Union was expressly sceptical on that point.[8]

In keeping with Norway's general approach and striving to prevent the development of bloc formations, the Norwegian negotiators in Paris advocated positioning the Marshall Aid within the UN system. Together with the Swedes, who were preoccupied with being able to maintain trade with Eastern Europe as they had done during the war, Norway argued that a dedicated, permanent organization should not be created. Norway felt there should be no competition with the UN organization for European reconstruction, the UN Economic Commission for Europe (UNECE). Moreover, the UN track would place the American initiative within a wider framework and might make it easier for Norway to continue its role as a bridge-builder between the blocs that had arisen, thus fulfilling the government's foreign-policy objective. The Norwegian proposal was rejected by the Americans and the other countries. They thought the UN system was far too broad and did not have the necessary mechanism to make regular decisions as to how the plan should be implemented.

The Minister of Foreign Affairs, Halvard Lange, further claimed that the 16 countries receiving the Marshall Aid did not form a natural economic entity.[9] That was directly at odds with the vision behind the American aid, but exactly as Carl Joachim Hambro claimed in the book *Crossroads of Conflict. European Peoples and Problems* from 1943.

The task for the Norwegian chief negotiator in Paris, Gunnar Jahn, was therefore: How could Norway say yes to the American money *without* "deviating" from the traditional Norwegian planned economy, *without* appearing to be an American ally, *without* weakening the UN's role and *without* challenging the Soviet Union's European interests?

7   H. Lie, *Skjebneår 1945-1950*, Oslo: Tiden, 1985, p. 203.
8   H.Ø. Pharo, "Bridgebuilding and reconstruction. Norway faces the Marshall Plan", *Scandinavian Journal of History*, May 1 (1-4), 1976, pp. 125-153.
9   N.A. Røhne, "De første skritt inn i Europa. Norsk Europa-politikk fra 1950", *Forsvarsstudier*, 5, 1989, p. 15.

The task was an impossible one. The Norwegian delegation therefore considered all proposals and conclusions from the meetings from every possible angle. Every time a consensus seemed to be forming around the table, they took the floor. Eventually, the British Chancellor of the Exchequer lost his patience and fired off previously cited questions as to whether Norway belonged to Western Europe. Most unusual for a polite and diplomatic Brit!

The US demands regarding economic cooperation

The economic situation was far worse for most other European countries, where the German occupation had wreaked much greater damage, and warfare and the allies' bombing had all but wiped out towns and villages. Only north Norway experienced anything similar. In Germany, every fourth home had been destroyed, and the gross national product had been reduced by 70 percent.

This was the situation as the US Minister of Foreign Affairs, George C. Marshall, described Europe in his speech to graduating students at Harvard University on 5 June 1947.[10] He pointed to the inability to rebuild society because all resources were being used to import food and goods, from the USA more or less. This deprived European countries of the opportunity to invest in necessary infrastructure, agriculture and industry. To cap it all, the long, icy-cold winter of 1946-1947 resulted in widespread hunger, chaos and desperation. The European economy was trapped in a vicious circle that could provide a breeding ground for the ideological counterpart to Fascism-Communism, Marshall told the American people.

America had come to Europe's rescue twice in 30 years, and half a million American lives had been lost.[11] The USA therefore demanded that the money be spent on creating lasting and irreversible links between

---

[10] George C. Marshall's speech on 5 June 1947. See http://www.oecd.org/general/themarshallplanspeechatharvarduniversity5june1947.htm.

[11] The number of American lives lost during the first and second world wars varies according to sources. The history learning site in GB and the *Encyclopaedia Britannica* both operate with 295,000 fallen American soldiers in WWII and about 125,000 in WWI. www.historylearningsite.co.uk.

the one-time warring enemies in order to avoid fresh war and conflict on the continent. The aid should not just help get Europe out of its acute distress: The money was to be used to establish pioneering cooperation across national borders and reduce the nation-states' sovereignty.[12] The Americans thought that lasting peace could only be ensured by entering into legally binding supranational cooperation. There must be no repeat of the situation after the First World War: in the 1930s Adolf Hitler had come to power precisely because the German and European economies collapsed and created chaos. People called for a strong leader with a dazzling ideology to get them out of their misery. That provided a hotbed for Nazism. A contributory factor to Hitler's path to power was the debt Germany was ordered to pay off after the First World War. If the Germans were to cope with repaying the war debt, they needed a surplus on the balance of trade, which is to say that they had to export more goods than they imported. If they could not manage it, the money would trickle out of the country and the authorities would have to put up taxes and duties in order to raise money to pay off their debt, which would choke the economy. So the Germans devalued the Deutsche Mark. German goods became cheaper overnight, and they were able to increase exports to France and the other countries around them. Then the money flowed in. Frenchmen and Britons gave them a taste of their own medicine in return, however: they devalued their own currencies in order to outdo German goods. In addition, the countries all introduced trade barriers and tariff rates that made trading difficult and expensive. Prices rose and led to hyperinflation, mass unemployment and gradually political chaos in the great majority of countries in thirties' Europe. The situation was best summed up by the well-known picture of the German who had to have a wheelbarrow full of money with him to buy a loaf of bread!

It was this scenario the Americans wished to prevent a repeat of. They desired new and closer political and economic cooperation between the countries. The Americans therefore demanded that those receiving aid reduce their customs barriers to allow trade between the countries. In addition, they wanted the countries to enter into supranational cooperation on strategic industry and raw materials.

---

[12]   D.P. Calleo, *The Imperious Economy*, Boston, Massachusetts: Harvard University Press, 1982.

Europe's integration process was a conscious and well thought-through American idea and strategy. However, it would prove clearly contrary to Norwegian foreign-policy objectives both before and after the Second World War.

In the USA, the Republicans had taken control of Congress in the by-elections of 1946. The Republicans had pledged to reduce public spending and conduct a new isolationist foreign policy, so many people took a less than positive view of the proposal to spend 5 percent of GNP to put bellicose Europe back on its feet. President Harry S. Truman, who had the idea of helping Europe, gave the task of launching that aid to the popular general and Minister of Foreign Affairs, George C. Marshall. Together, Truman and Marshall spent considerable effort and several months trying to persuade Congress.[13] In February 1948, when the Marshall Plan Aid was being debated in Congress, the Communists in Czechoslovakia overthrew the government in power and assumed control. The Prague coup showed the world the Soviet Union's true intentions. The arguments that the Marshall Plan would contribute to preventing the progress of Communism in Europe thus gained ground and Congress members passed the Economic Cooperation Act of 1948.[14] When the Americans put their money on the table at Château de la Muette in autumn 1948, negotiations about how to distribute and use it could begin.

Norwegian "yes" to the Marshall Plan

The mood in Norwegian political circles also began to turn. Events in Czechoslovakia contributed to undermining faith in the idea of the bridge-builder's role. Participating in the negotiations and discussions between countries at Château de la Muette gradually provided Norwegian representatives from all ministries better insight into and appreciation of the way European cooperation worked in practice. The organization was dubbed the Organization for European Economic Cooperation (OEEC). The negotiations required active Norwegian involvement.

---

[13] *Ibid.*, pp. 16, 20-21. See also http://marshallfoundation.org/library/documents/ Chapter_2.pdf and http://usa.usembassy.de/etexts/marshall/pam-blu.htm.

[14] See http://www.marshallfoundation.org/library/documents/Marshall_Plan/Reports/ Foreign_Assistance Act_of_1948.pdf.

That helped alter the traditional Norwegian approach, which was based on having to protect national interests. In rapid succession, Norwegian delegates were forced to adopt a position on the proposals for cooperating with the other countries around the table. The discussions furnished the Norwegian government with altogether necessary ammunition for the political debate at home on the advantages and drawbacks of accepting the American aid. The group pressure, or peer pressure, from the meeting venues at Château de la Muette worked.

A Gallup poll from 1948 showed that 85 percent of Norwegians who were aware of the Marshall Plan wanted Norway to take part. The same went for 50 percent of the members of Norway's Communist Party. The Marshall Plan enjoyed great support among people.[15]

Finally, Norway and the other countries accepted the Marshall Plan and lent their support to taking part in the OEEC. The neutrality line in the Gerhardsen government lost the internal battle in the Labour Party. Norway's economic recovery was able to gather speed along a financial course plotted chiefly from the château in the 16th arrondissement of Paris.

During the years 1948 to 1952 Europe experienced the strongest economic growth in its history. Hunger and poverty disappeared and were replaced with employment and welfare. Norway came out of the Marshall Plan distribution particularly favourably. Measured per inhabitant, Norway received more money than any other country in Europe.[16] The support for Norway totalled 439 million dollars over the four years the Marshall Plan was dispensed.[17] That was more than four times the 100 million dollars the Ministry of Finance thought Norway needed in April 1947. Norway received about 3 billion kroner, equivalent to roughly 57 billion kroner in today's money. Norway was the supreme winner of the American initiative which the government had expended great ingenuity and effort to obstruct.

---

[15]   T. Bergh and H. Ø. Pharo (ed.), *Vekst og velstand. Norsk politisk historie 1945-65*, Oslo: Universitetsforlaget, 1981, p. 192.

[16]   S. Sommerfelt, pp. 86, 156 and 6 in M. Hertzberg Erichsen and T. Halvorsen, *Marshallplanen og norsk offisiell statistikk*, 1997. https://www.ssb.no/a/histstat/not/not_9877.pdf.

[17]   M. Hertzberg Erichsen and T. Halvorsen, *Marshallplanen og norsk offisiell statistikk*, p. 3. See https://www.ssb.no/a/histstat/not/not_9877.pdf.

Minister of Foreign Affairs Lange even said at the Labour Party Conference in 1949 that "the USA, generally thought of as the world stronghold of private capitalism, had lent its support to joint economic planning in Europe which in many ways is in keeping with our Socialist planned economic principles".[18] The turnaround might appear to be complete. In total, the Americans paid 17 billion dollars for the reconstruction of Europe, mostly as a gift. In 2014 this was equivalent to 160 billion dollars.

False hopes and realities

To the outside world the government's tone was still different, oddly enough, because although Norway had finally agreed to take part in the new European collaborative organization in order to receive the Marshall Aid, there was still great scepticism surrounding the European project in Norwegian political circles. During a visit to New York on 1 December 1949 the Minister of Foreign Affairs, Halvard Lange, gave a lecture with the same anti-European outlook as previously. The title of the lecture was "European unification. False hopes and realities". Lange still maintained that Europe did not form a natural economic or political entity.[19] Lange's line in foreign policy appeared to be clearly anti-European and in opposition to the American vision of a united Europe. Nor did it sound particularly grateful to the country that had donated 5 percent of its gross national product to reconstruct Europe.

However, the Paris negotiations on the Marshall Plan and the gradual distribution of the American money would alter Lange's view of Europe and European integration. After Norway took a very reluctant step into the OEEC and was forced to actively take part in the extensive committee work where all the countries sat around together drawing up a road map to reconstruct society, political perceptions also changed. A considerable share of the work would turn out to be involved with technical and economic cooperation, and the political dimension was not shaping up as the government had feared. There was a complete sea

---

[18] Minutes of the Norwegian Labour Party (DNA's) conference in 1949, p. 123.
[19] N.A. Røhne, "De første skritt inn i Europa. Norsk Europa-politikk fra 1950", *Forsvarsstudier* 5, side 15, 1989.

change, and the Norwegian government went from throwing spanners into the works for the Marshall Plan to actively pushing for the OEEC's remit to be expanded and strengthened. In addition, the government was pleased with the contact and links to the USA and Canada, which gave it an Atlantic feel and thus accentuated it as an economic parallel to NATO.

"Reluctantly and grudgingly, therefore, Norway took its first step towards European cooperation by participating in the Marshall Plan organization (OEEC)",[20] writes Nils A. Røhne in one of his foremost studies of early Norwegian policy on Europe. Or as described by Rune Slagstad in the book *De nasjonale strateger [*"The National Strategists"*]*: "The Marshall Plan was not immediately granted a hearty reception by the government."[21] You can say that again! The total reversal in Norwegian attitude stemmed from the experience the Norwegian negotiators gleaned from the negotiations in Paris. The reports home from ambassador Arne Skaug suggested that Norway was not alone in the OEEC. Several countries were struggling with the same problems: the dilemmas between protecting national markets and industries, and opening up to competition and economies of scale.

Norway went from being the country asking for the least economic support to becoming the country that received most money per inhabitant. During the period 1948-1952 Norway received aid from the USA to a value of 57 billion kroner measured in 2013 terms.[22]

From a historical perspective, it looks undeniably as if it was far-sighted American politics coupled with great economic incentives that lured the Norwegian political milieu into joining cooperation in which planned economy, protectionism and the idea of the bridge-builder's role were put to one side. Norway took the step towards a rather more open and dynamic market economy.

Lange, the Minister of Foreign Affairs, who had previously displayed scepticism towards Europe, gradually became more convinced of the

---

[20] *Ibid.*, p. 13.

[21] R. Slagstad, *De nasjonale strateger*, Oslo: Pax forlag, 1998, p. 232.

[22] T. Rolf, "Oljealder 1965-95", i *Norsk utenrikspolitikks historie*. Vol. 6. Oslo: Universitetsforlaget, 1997.

need for European integration. For the last seven years of his life, he led the European Movement in Norway.

The OECD as an arena for new cooperation

OEEC, the organization Norway was reluctant to take part in, turned out to be crucial to the development of new European collaborative organizations. It was around the table at Château de la Muette that the countries' governments discussed projects for defence cooperation, the Coal and Steel Union, and nuclear cooperation. In 1961 the organization was turned into the Organization for Economic Cooperation and Development (OECD), which now has 34 members from all over the world. The OECD has acted as a think-tank for Western industrialized countries since the war and as a discussion forum for authorities on political initiatives and experiences. Altogether seminal Norwegian political reforms originate from the OECD. Political concepts like "active labour market policy", "lifelong learning", green taxes and the Labour and Welfare Organization/Administration (NAV) Reform were not conceived in Oslo's equivalent of Whitehall. They were evolved through discussions between like-minded industrialized countries at Château de la Muette. The same goes for the body of thought behind the Norwegian liberalization of the energy, telecommunications and aviation markets at the end of the 1980s and start of the 1990s, which was introduced by the EU and the majority of other countries in Europe later on. In 1991, it was the OECD countries that arrived at the conclusion that the EU cooperation should orchestrate the reconstruction of the poor countries of Central and Eastern Europe. This, again, was in keeping with the American vision that the organization and reconstruction of Europe should be undertaken first and foremost by the Europeans themselves.

"Before Norway goes under" – NATO membership

In parallel with the Marshall Plan, the Americans took the initiative to set up the North Atlantic Treaty Organization (NATO). The Soviet-sponsored coup in Prague, the Berlin Blockade and the Soviets' pressure on Finland to accept a "neutrality agreement" meant that many people were pointing to Norway as the next victim of Soviet expansionism.

The famous telegram from the British Foreign Secretary, Ernest Bevin, to his American colleague George Marshall, gave the signal to set the NATO negotiations in train "before Norway goes under".[23] As Haakon Lie relates in his book *Skjebneår 1945-1950 ["Those Fateful Years 1945-1950"]*: "We were caught with our trousers down once. That was quite enough!"[24]

Three reasons are generally highlighted for Norway joining this alliance. Firstly, the war had shown that Norway's geographical location was more exposed than previously thought. Norway was no longer on the fringes of Europe. Secondly, 9 April had taught us that a defence force could not be mobilized the same day the enemy was on the doorstep. Assistance had to be planned in peace time if it was to work in wartime. Thirdly, the Norwegians had clearly realized that Norway could not defend itself.

The post-war years saw a number of exploratory contacts being made with Sweden and Denmark to look into the possibilities of setting up a Scandinavian or Nordic alliance, but Swedish demands concerning Norwegian neutrality were not acceptable to Great Britain and the USA. Reports from my uncle, Paal Frisvold, who was then a special military adviser at the Norwegian Embassy in Stockholm, flagged up an additional factor: The Swedes' inability or unwillingness to take part in funding the Norwegian defence. He later said that the lack of economic support from Sweden was one of the main reasons for the Nordic defence cooperation being unworkable. The Americans, by contrast, offered to finance large parts of the Norwegian defence, including industrial cooperation that created thousands of Norwegian jobs. The Marshall Plan had proved that the Americans meant business and had the economic capacity to supply Norway with arms and ammunition.[25]

There was great fear, however, of the consequences of no longer being able to act as bridge-builder. In practice, this had consisted of keeping Norway out of binding cooperation with other countries in Western Europe. The Soviet pressure Norway had been facing at that

---

[23]   H. Lie, *Skjebneår 1945-1950*, Oslo: Tiden, 1985, p. 275.
[24]   *Ibid.*, p. 282.
[25]   K. Skogrand, "Cash and Cannons; Norway, Denmark and the US aid programmes 1947-1952", *IFS/info*, No. 2, 1998.

time gave the impression that the Soviet Union would feel threatened if Western Europe did not remain fragmented. Its touchiness about the Soviet Union contributed to splitting the Norwegian Labour Party. For a long time Gerhardsen seemed to doubt the foundation for Norway's traditional bridge-building philosophy, which extended back to 1905. Lange, on the other hand, was heavily influenced by the Soviet liquidation of his good friend and colleague Jan Masaryk, who back then had been Minister of Foreign Affairs in Czechoslovakia. A group led by Minister Lange and former head of Milorg and then Minister of Defence Jens Christian Hauge launched an all-out campaign to mobilize key people throughout society. Among other things, the Norwegian Confederation of Trade Unions (LO), the National Defence and industry made up a broad-based, hard-hitting coalition; and after long and impassioned political debates in the *Storting* Norway eventually acceded to the establishment of NATO on 4 April 1949.

The Council of Europe and the European Court of Human Rights

Norwegian participation in the Marshall Plan and NATO did not bring about a metamorphosis in Norway's attitude towards European and international cooperation either. The same old scepticism reared its head when France suggested setting up the Council of Europe in 1949. Above all, the intention was to establish a forum where national parliamentarians could get together to discuss issues related to democracy and human rights. The Council of Europe, which is now led by Secretary-General Thorbjørn Jagland, is Europe's leading human rights organization, with 47 member states. They have all ratified the European Convention on Human Rights and committed themselves to binding standards for human rights, democracy and the state based on the rule of law. The Council of Europe monitors compliance with these obligations by means of various supervisory schemes and is given credit for having put controversial political issues like equality and the rights of homosexuals and transsexuals on the agenda in Russia and other Eastern European countries.

Winston Churchill was also a driving force in establishing the Council of Europe, but when the French initiative arrived in Oslo, it was received with a very negative attitude on the part of the Norwegian government. Together with Great Britain, Norway argued against the organization having any form of supranational cooperation whatsoever. That applied particularly to the proposal to set up a self-contained court of human rights. Norway was unable to accept that the court would have precedence over national courts. The government strongly opposed Turkish and Greek involvement. As in the context of NATO, Norway was actively trying to keep the Mediterranean countries out. Norway, to use Lange's words, was "sceptical about plans for integration with the Mediterranean countries".[26] But once again the pressure was set to become too great. Norway could do nothing but capitulate. Under strong American pressure the British agreed to take part on condition that the Council of Europe was to be "a strict intergovernmental collaboration without any form of supranationality".[27] That made the government's job vis-à-vis the *Storting* simpler. Nowadays Norway can bask in the reflected glory of being one of the Council of Europe's ten founding member states. The Court of Human Rights in Strasbourg is now considered the world's top court in interpreting the practical importance of UN human rights. Norway, incidentally, has received adverse rulings in Strasbourg several times and has amended its legislation accordingly.

The attempt at Nordic cooperation – *the Nordic Council and NORDØK*

During the period after the Second World War, several initiatives were taken to link the Nordic countries together. Early on, it became clear that the countries were too far apart to reach any collective understanding on security policy. The war had brought Norway closer to Great Britain and the USA, and it gradually became natural for Norway and Denmark to affiliate themselves with NATO. Sweden wanted to preserve her neutrality, while Finland was "Finlandized", i.e. pressured into signing an agreement with the Soviet Union on foreign

---

[26]   H. Lange, *Norsk utenrikspolitikk siden 1945*, Oslo: Johan Grundt Tanums forlag, 1952, pp. 135-136.
[27]   B. Bredrup Knudsen, *Den nye Europa-debatten*, Oslo: Cappelen, 1989, p. 391.

and defence policy. During the discussions at Château de la Muette, as early as 1948, a joint Nordic Committee for Economic Cooperation was created. The aim was to look into the possibilities of establishing a Nordic customs union. Great was the disappointment when Norway's Minister of Foreign Affairs, Halvard Lange, had to pull Norway out of the negotiations because Norwegian industry and agriculture would not be able to survive the competition from Sweden and Denmark.[28] The committee had already been decommissioned by 1950. The Nordic dimension cropped up a number of times in the 1950s, but was continually gunned down by Norway, which did not wish for any binding cooperation.[29]

In 1952 the Nordic Council was set up. Even this organization was destined to encounter great resistance from the right-of-centre parties in the *Storting*, which formed a not inconsiderable minority. There was no such resistance from the Danish Parliament, *Folketinget*, or the Swedish one, *Riksdagen*.[30] Norway wished to satisfy itself that the Nordic Council would have no element of supranationality, and therefore made sure that no cabinet members would have the right to vote, and no permanent secretariat function was created for the presidency either.[31]

From the creation of the Nordic labour market in 1951, it took three years till the *Storting* ratified the agreement. The Agrarian Party, later to become the Centre Party, was particularly opposed to the agreement on the free movement of labour between the Nordic countries, but in the end it did not manage to stop the agreement being ratified in 1954. The agreement on a free labour market was trail-blazing. Two years later agreement was reached on social security rights. And sure enough, it was far less of an ambition and a financial commitment than a customs union intended to dismantle customs barriers on industrial products, food and farming produce.

---

[28] N. Engelschiøn, *Norway and European integration: 1945-1972*, Masters dissertation, Reading: University of Reading, 1992, p. 33.

[29] H. Pharo, K.E. Eriksen and T. Berg, *Vekst og velstand. Norsk politisk historie 1945-1964*, Oslo: Universitetsforlaget, 1981, p. 171.

[30] T.B. Olesen, "Den europæiske utfordring. EU, EEA og nordisk samarbejde – i historisk belysing", *Europautredningen (The Norwegian Europe Review)*, subreport 12, 2011, p. 10.

[31] *Ibid.*

Many people claim that more than 90 years of union with Sweden were the most important cause of the resistance to supranational Nordic cooperation. The reality, however, was more complex. The cause was the fear that Norwegian industry and agriculture would not cope with competing with our neighbours.

In 1968 one last desperate attempt was made to put in place large-scale Nordic cooperation. Denmark took the initiative for NORDØK, a plan to create customs frontiers and establish close industrial and economic cooperation. The plan also involved a proposal for common decision-making institutions, fisheries and agricultural policy, something once again totally unacceptable to Norway.[32] Eventually, therefore, the parties agreed on a much looser form of cooperation. Finland was not allowed to take part in NORDØK by the Soviet Union. The Danes, who had been worn down by the Norwegian opposition to binding economic cooperation like the customs union, preferred to turn to the EC, the French veto against British membership having been rescinded. Hence the whole NORDØK project collapsed.

Fear of being outcompeted by Danish agriculture and Swedish industry was at the root of an initiative to get the Norwegian government to block the plan for a Nordic customs union in 1947-1950, 1954-1958 and 1967-1969. And the present-day EEA Agreement is not a customs union either, having kept both farming and processed agricultural produce outside of the free trade area.

When the *Storting* opposed the proposal for a European free trade area within the framework of the OEEC as well as the proposal for Nordic cooperation, the Danes and the Swedes began to look for another way. The Danish historian Thorsten Borring Olesen points to Norway's repeatedly negative attitude towards Nordic cooperation as one of the main reasons for the Danish government turning towards EC cooperation.[33]

Attending on behalf of the Swedish government, Olof Palme also vented some form of frustration when, in 1971, at a meeting of the

[32] K.E. Eriksen, "Norge og Norden, Samarbeid og kollisjon," Nato 50-år, Norwegian Atlantic Committee (DNAK) (www.atlanterhavskomiteen.no).
[33] H. Pharo, K.E. Eriksen and T. Berg, *Vekst og velstand. Norsk politisk historie 1945-1964*, Oslo: Universitetsforlaget, 1981, p. 171.

Nordic Council of Ministers, he uttered: "Nordic cooperation's path to success is flanked by grandiose failures."

As a means of making amends for its inability to establish binding economic cooperation, Nordic cooperation over the past 40 years has attached importance to entirely non-binding cooperation as an exchange of political experiences and softer areas such as research, teaching, art, film and language. Nordic cooperation has become a strategically important arena for Norway, because it provides opportunities both for networking and for presenting and winning sympathy for Norwegian views on the many issues Norway has with the EU.

The lack of political superstructure in the Nordic region contributed to the absence of any political anchorage and inadequate support for important projects on economic cooperation. Thus visionary Nordic projects like, for example, the joint Nordic satellite project Nordsat, the Volvo agreement on an exchange agreement between the Norwegian state and Volvo, and the Telenor and Telia cooperation broke down. The political vigour was lacking to motivate players to raise the bar and overcome cultural and economic problems.[34] The 2000s saw the promotion of a number of initiatives to bring gas on stream from Norway to Poland via Sweden. In the wake of many reports, the Stavanger-based initiative Austerled, later the Greenland project and the Scandinavian ScanLed were found to be too expensive, too long and too commercially uncertain. There was a lack of political gravitas and support as well as the ability to place Norwegian economic interests in a geopolitical context. The Swedes turned to Denmark and Germany instead. Only the Polish authorities pointed to the dawning uncertainty surrounding Europe's dependence on importing large volumes of gas from Russia. This problem was highlighted by the EU even in the 2006 green paper.[35] Seeing as we do today how Poland and large parts of Central and Eastern Europe wish to reduce their dependence on Russian gas imports, the gas pipeline from Norway to Poland would have been a political and economic success for Norway and Europe. It could have given the government a valuable entry point to the Polish authorities, who are among the top players in Europe today. Poland certainly used

---

[34] *Ibid.*, p. 11.

[35] A European strategy for sustainable, competitive and secure energy, European Commission (COM 2006) Final.

the dialogues with Norway as a negotiating card with Russia too. Later on, the Poles would contract with Qatar to supply liquefied natural gas by ship to a new port facility in Gdansk.

René Pleven and the idea of a European army

In addition to NATO cooperation, a number of European countries spoke out in favour of an independent defence cooperation under European political leadership. The objective was to find a political solution to how to involve West Germany, not yet in NATO at that point, in the defence of Western Europe.

The idea of a European army was fostered by the French Minister of Defence, René Pleven, in October 1950 and supported by people including Winston Churchill. It met with fierce resistance in many European countries, including Norway, primarily because no one wanted German remilitarization, but after the Korean War broke out in 1950 that resistance turned and the agreement on a "European Defence Community" (EDC) was signed in Paris in May 1952. In spite of American support for the Pleven Plan and Norwegian involvement in the Korean War, the government did not modify its opposition to the plan. However, when it became clear that German participation would be necessary for NATO's capability to defend Norway, the government threw itself into following the negotiations "with interest".[36]

German remilitarization and participation in defence cooperation was premature and ended in crisis.

The initiative died a death in Pleven's own national assembly, which voted down the proposal in August 1954. Norway was able to breathe a sigh of relief and put the debate on involvement in European defence cooperation aside. Two years later France and Great Britain sent troops to Egypt to liberate the Suez Canal. The USA was not consulted and gave them no support because they were afraid of escalating the situation with Soviet participation. The action failed, both militarily and politically, and the French and the British withdrew some months

---

[36]   N.A. Røhne, "De første skritt inn i Europa. Norsk Europa-politikk fra 1950", *Forsvarsstudier* 5, 1989, p. 23.

later, putting a complete stop to European defence cooperation right up to the French-British summit meeting in Saint-Malo in 1999.

In the *Storting* the chairman of the Parliamentary Foreign Committee, the Labour Party's Finn Moe, claimed that "Norway also shared some of the responsibility for the difficulties in the EDC negotiations. If, together with Great Britain and Denmark, Norway had taken a more positive view of EDC cooperation, the crisis could have been averted".[37]

The European Coal and Steel Union

Another initiative from the negotiating table in conference room C at Château de la Muette was the French proposal for a union of its own between France, Germany, the Benelux countries and Italy. The idea was to set up a joint administrative body for the most important raw materials, coal and steel. The French felt they had lost some of the control over the reconstruction of Germany through the Marshall Plan and wanted to make sure the German coal and steel industry did not rise up again as a threat. The French Minister of Foreign Affairs, Robert Schuman, presented the proposal in a famous speech on 9 May 1950.

Norway's reaction was lukewarm initially, especially as the proposal bore the hallmark of supranational cooperation. The Minister of Foreign Affairs, Halvard Lange, nevertheless took a positive view of the political importance of being able to anchor down Germany like a Western European country. After Great Britain had decided not to take part, Norway put all interests aside. Norway's delegation at the OEEC in Paris quite simply did not assign priority to sending home information about developments in the negotiations between the six countries.[38] Once again the Norwegian Ministry of Foreign Affairs took a reluctant view of the whole project, doubting whether it would even "be possible to accomplish anything whatsoever".[39] That assessment proved to be entirely misjudged. On 18 April 1950, the six countries

---

[37]   N.A. Røhne, "De første skritt inn i Europa. Norsk Europa-politikk fra 1950", *Forsvarsstudier* 5, side 25, 1989.

[38]   Norwegian Ministry of Foreign Affairs 52.2/23. N.A. Røhne, "De første skritt inn i Europa. Norsk Europa-politikk fra 1950", *Forsvarsstudier* 5, 1989, p. 18.

[39]   *Ibid.*

signed the historic agreement on supranational cooperation regarding the administration of coal and steel, including trading, pricing and wage levels. Rolf Andvord, Norway's ambassador to the OEEC, still refused to drop his scepticism and reported home that there was no cause for concern all the same. He claimed that in all probability the countries would not win approval for the salient items. The Coal and Steel Union, he said, would never be ratified.

The German chancellor Konrad Adenauer later described the European Coal and Steel Union as a decisive turning point in Europe's development. The agreement came into force on 25 July 1952, after ratification processes had been completed in all six countries. It was only two years later that the Norwegian government decided to form a committee to evaluate the possible consequences of the Coal and Steel Union for Norway.

Meanwhile, Minister Lange went to London to look up his British colleague Anthony Eden. Lange expressed the view that Norway might suffer if the Coal and Steel Union managed the resources between the six member states without taking Norwegian needs into consideration. Eden promised that Great Britain would ensure that neither British nor Norwegian interests were compromised. Not till seven months later, on 11 October 1954, did the committee present its assessment. On that basis, the government's evaluation concluded that "there were not strong enough grounds for Norway at the present time to take steps to seek to achieve a closer association with the Community".[40] The government added that the picture would change if Great Britain were to endorse the agreement – which the British did not do, or at any rate not this time around.

The European Free Trade Association (EFTA), Britain's answer to the Coal and Steel Union

Once the European Coal and Steel Union between the six continental countries got off the ground, the British tabled a competing project based on free trade between the countries involved with the Marshall Plan.

---

[40]   Norwegian Ministry of Foreign Affairs, 52/23, Vol. 11, "Norges forhold til Kull- og stålunionen – utredning fra interdepartemental utvalg", 11.10.54.

Expert groups were set up at Château de la Muette in 1956 and the following year concluded that the project was possible. Seen through today's eyes, it was very similar to the first proposal submitted to Jacques Delors for two-tier European economic cooperation between the EU and EFTA, only with the same decision-making mechanisms. This was a proposal to which Norway's Minister of Foreign Affairs lent his full support, particularly in light of the change of heart which the *Storting* and government had had in the face of the Marshall Plan and Norwegian participation in the OEEC. But the *Storting's* foreign, finance and industry committees did not agree. Again, the argument centred around a weak Norwegian economy with fragile industry and farming that would not stand up to competition from neighbouring countries. In the two years before the popularly elected representatives considered the British proposal for a European free trade area, Norway's relationship with Europe was barely mentioned in the *Storting*, and was not discussed in anything like satisfactory fashion. Nils A. Røhne writes that "the popularly elected were prepared neither politically nor psychologically, therefore, to lend their support to a proposal for concrete European cooperation virtually overnight."[41]

As Minister of Trade, Arne Skaug, said of France's negotiating position: "They are out for [...] a political assembly, while we are out for increased trade, and nothing more."[42] Thus the debate ended. The *Storting* added that Norway was happy to take part in further negotiations but not to commit to any concrete objectives. Norway would listen in, not take part. Exactly as in 1908, 1929, 1940, 1948 and 1952.

Against the EEC's customs union

Creation of the EFTA cooperation got underway in 1958. The basic premiss was that the EFTA countries were to form a joint arena to negotiate on membership of the EEC. If that failed, the countries were to agree a limited free trade area. Even from such humble beginnings, EFTA

---

[41] N.A. Røhne, "De første skritt inn i Europa. Norsk Europa-politikk fra 1950", *Forsvarsstudier* 5, 1989, p. 49.
[42] *Ibid.*, p. 53.

62

was intended to act as a stepping stone to Europe's main cooperation.[43] Right after EFTA was set up in 1960, the Americans convened a meeting in Paris between the EEC[44] and the EFTA countries. The aim was to look at possible cooperation between the two blocs and avoid a schism between the Western European countries. The President of the EEC Commission, Walter Hallstein, had proposed further dismantling of the customs barriers between the EEC countries and a collective external customs tariff. The Norwegian government thought a joint customs union between the EEC countries would take its toll on Norwegian economic interests. Norway also maintained that the EEC's plans would lead to an additional economic and political split between Eastern and Western Europe. Norway therefore asked the USA and Canada for understanding and sympathy for the Norwegian wish to counter the EEC's plans.[45] Hallstein's initiative was passed by the EEC countries anyway, with no reference to Norway and the other EFTA countries' problem. This outcome came as a surprise to the government, and when the British decided to apply for membership, the government saw no way out but to follow suit. Thus the EEC countries were instrumental in effecting the government's and the Norwegian Ministry of Foreign Affairs' change of heart and eventual support for application for membership of the EEC.

As in 1947, few others shared the Norwegian view of building a bridge between east and west, at the expense of closer mutual binding cooperation.

Great Britain does an about-turn on the EEC question

The news of the British application for membership of the EEC came as a bombshell to the Norwegian political debate.[46] One can only wonder why the powers that be in the Norwegian Ministry of Foreign

---

[43]   N.A. Røhne, "De første skritt inn i Europa. Norsk Europa-politikk fra 1950", *Forsvarsstudier* 5, 1989, p. 57.

[44]   In this book EEC is used instead of "EØF" (the equivalent Norwegian abbreviation).

[45]   N.A. Røhne, "De første skritt inn i Europa. Norsk Europa-politikk fra 1950", *Forsvarsstudier* 5, 1989, p. 61.

[46]   R. Tamnes and K.E. "Eriksen, Norge og Nato under den kalde krigen", i *Nato 50 år. Norsk sikkerhetspolitikk med Nato gjennom 50 år*, Norwegian Atlantic Committee (DNAK), p. 25.

Affairs and the government had settled for the EFTA solution without particularly realizing what the British generally wanted: membership of the EEC. Halvard Lange even travelled to the Foreign Office to obtain a guarantee that Norway's interests would be safeguarded if Great Britain were to change sides. Political Norway was totally unprepared for a debate on European politics, and Gerhardsen had no choice but to try and keep the debate under wraps until after the general election in autumn 1961. But by August the debate was already mounting. First the debate revolved around whether it was even feasible for Norway to cede sovereignty to an international organization. In that case Norway would have to amend Section 93 of its constitution on the cession of sovereignty. It took three votes. The lines of conflict were the same in 1961 as in 1948 over the Marshall Plan, in 1949 over the Nordic Customs Union and the Council of Europe, and in 1956 over a European free trade area within the OEEC: The left side of the Labour Party, the Centre Party, parts of the Christian Democrats and the Liberal Party of Norway put the cession-of-sovereignty argument on hold, while in reality they were concerned with shielding the markets from outside competition. On the other side were the majority of the Labour Party and the Conservative Party of Norway (*Høyre*).

It was during this debate that the motion to hold a consultative referendum was passed, spearheaded by the Liberal Party and the Centre Party. For the Liberal Party this was a purely tactical ploy. It allowed the party to lift the membership issue out of the party programme and thus avoid a break-up, something the party failed to do ten years later. It is precisely the same line of argument used by the Progress Party today: that the EU question should not be decided by the *Storting*, but by the people, and therefore has no rightful place in the party's programme for participating in the *Storting*. Adopting clever tactics, the Centre Party advanced the argument that this was not just a matter of trade interests but of principles concerning the cession of sovereignty.[47] The Conservatives (*Høyre*) and Labour were opposed to having to hold a referendum at first. Gradually, however, the Labour Party warmed to the idea, while the Conservative Party dropped its resistance.

---

[47] K.E. Eriksen and H.Ø. Pharo, *Kald krig og internasjonalisering 1949-1965*, Oslo: Universitetsforlaget, 1997, p. 334.

The fateful decision was taken eleven years before the actual referendum took place. That gave capable people on the No-side the time and means to organize the opposition. This must have been one of the most strategically important decisions the Conservative Party and the Labour Party have ever taken for Norway. NATO membership, a common Nordic labour market and passport union, and the EEA were all passed by the *Storting*. If these matters had been put out to referendum, it is far from certain that a majority would have been obtained; and Norway would have found herself totally isolated. On the other hand, referenda on membership of NATO and the Nordic Council, for example, could have provided a host of valuable insights and debates in society. They could have enhanced people's appreciation of the significance and the advantages of international cooperation which they later took for granted. Instead, it came to pass as Per Kleppe wrote: "Much of what was hammered home to us over the years in order to reinforce solidarity and loyalty among the populus was now being used to argue against binding cooperation with other nations."[48]

Gerhardsen's yes

In his New Year's speech to usher in 1962, the Prime Minister, Einar Gerhardsen, set great store by the impending negotiations on EEC membership. All the reviews by all the ministries indicated that Norway must not remain outside the EEC. He rounded off the speech thus: "It is an important and difficult decision we now face, and it is no wonder that different views are being voiced. However, if the point of this exchange is to elucidate and inform, it must be businesslike."[49]

In January 1963, the French President Charles de Gaulle vetoed British membership of the EEC, thereby closing the door on Norway too, and the debate over Norwegian membership could thus be conveniently kicked into the long grass. Great Britain, followed in turn by Ireland, Denmark and Norway, re-applied for membership in 1967, which de Gaulle also opposed. Interestingly, the *Storting* voted by an

---

[48] P. Kleppe, *Norges vei til Europa*, Oslo: Aschehoug, 1989, p. 14.
[49] O. Solumsmoen and O. Larssen (ed.), *Med Einar Gerhardsen gjennom 20 år*, Oslo: Tiden, 1967, pp. 177-179.

overwhelming majority to apply for EEC membership in 1967: 136 voted in favour, only 13 against.

The people's first no

French President Charles de Gaulle resigned in 1969 after losing a referendum in the wake of the student riots. In the process some of the traditional French scepticism and fear of Great Britain's and the USA's Anglo-Saxon influence disappeared. De Gaulle had himself been touched by this during the Second World War when, among other things, he was not allowed to take part in the summit meeting in Yalta between Roosevelt, Stalin and Churchill, who divided Europe up between them. De Gaulle's successor, Georges Pompidou, welcomed the British to the EEC, and Great Britain immediately applied for membership, as had been on the cards for a long time. Ireland, Denmark and Norway followed. In 1970 the *Storting* submitted Norway's application. Once again there was a clear majority among Norway's popularly elected: 132 to 17 votes.

The Danish Prime Minister, Anker Jørgensen, contacted his Norwegian colleague Trygve Bratteli and asked nicely whether Norway might hold a referendum before Denmark. He thought the Danes might need a "Norwegian nudge" in order to grasp the gravity of the matter.

The Norwegian EC debate was an excruciating one that sowed deep discord and division throughout the country, among families, friends and colleagues. It was Norway's 1968 revolt, hand in hand with the Peace Movement, anti-Vietnam War, anti-USA, the Temperance Movement, environmental activists, farmers' organizations and all the opposing national forces. It was a political minefield in which both the Labour Party and the Liberal Party were split. The dissenters from the Labour Party during the NATO debate, the Socialist People's Party (later the Socialist Liberal Party), had fresh wind in their sails, and the Liberal Party was split in two with the formation of the Liberal People's Party. Norwegian society experienced a cold civil war. In the same way as the EU dispute 22 years later, the No-side was much more intense and down-to-earth in its organization and rhetoric than the Yes-side. Gerhardsen's call for a businesslike exchange was soon forgotten. The slogans tell their own story: The Yes-side used "Yes to the EC", while the No-side conceived the ingenious phrase "No to selling Norway!", making people believe that it was all about selling the country out wholesale to foreigners. It had little to do with reality. In reality, it was the converse.

Through the government's "Pension Fund Global", aka the Petroleum Fund, Norway now owns 8 percent of all shares in Europe and many prestigious properties in Europe's capitals.

The left flank of the Labour Party had set up a popular movement even by 1961, followed by the farmers' organizations the year after. According to the paper *Dagbladet's* scrutiny of the archives for the KGB's chief archivist, Vasili Mitrokhin, these groups are supposed to have received financial backing from the KGB.[50] In light of the fact that the Soviet Union strove to neutralize all forms of Scandinavian, Nordic and European integration from the beginning of the Cold War, this is quite likely.

The No-side won by 53.5 percent to 46.5 percent – a political earthquake of the kind which together with the 1994 referendum is deeply ingrained in everyone who lived through it. It is an important contributory factor in the political leadership of modern-day Norway not wishing for a new debate. As ex-Prime Minister Jens Stoltenberg said when he met the press during the Social Democrats' party conference in Berlin in 2011: "I shall never use any political ammunition on a new EU fight."

Also against the UN's maritime organization

In 1948 the USA and Great Britain took the initiative for an international convention designed to create the UN's consultative maritime body, IMCO (International Maritime Consultative Committee, later the International Maritime Organization (IMO)).

The Americans and the British had experienced the need for coordination and security at sea from the allies' extensive collaboration on shipping during the war. The government in Oslo, influenced by the Norwegian Shipowners' Association, opposed the proposal. For Norway's part, it was important to return to the pre-war regime, when no one could assert rules and standards on the open sea by dint of

---

[50]   KGB archives: KGB støttet nei-bevegelsen, *Dagbladet*, 14 August 2014.

established custom.[51] At that time Norway was the world's third-largest shipping nation and had no desire to get into a predicament where countries with a smaller navy that prioritized the rights of mariners or coastal areas could outnumber Norway. The principle of the freedom of the sea took precedence over global security standards, mariners' rights and environmental risk. In the *Storting* debate Carl Joachim Hambro thought that international cooperation could lead to reduced Norwegian competitiveness, as it might give other nations access to Norwegian know-how and technology.[52]

Together with Sweden, Norway went as far as to exert pressure on Japan not to ratify the agreement to create the IMCO. The plan was to avoid large shipping nations like Japan and Greece ratifying the agreement so that it would never come into effect. Norway could then hide behind the other countries and say: "It wasn't our fault."

The stratagem was discovered by the Americans, who felt compelled to fight fire with fire. Unless Norway changed her attitude to setting up the IMCO, they would make sure she would not get an executive position in the new organization. After the Japanese ratification in spring 1958 the convention came into force. On 29 December 1958, ten years after the founding conference in Geneva, the *Storting* ratified the convention to create the IMCO. Norway was then one of the very last countries in the world to ratify the convention. Pressure from America, together with the arguments put to people including the chair of the *Storting*'s Standing Committee on Foreign Affairs, Finn Moe, about Norway's scope for exerting influence from within, prevailed over the scepticism of Hambro and the others in the national conservative group. A supplementary declaration of their own to the effect that the IMCO was not allowed to extend its mandate beyond cooperation in purely technical fields was finally dropped on the recommendation of the Minister of Foreign Affairs. We eventually came on side in this field too.

---

[51] M. Malmer, *Norge og IMCO*, Masters thesis, Oslo: University of Oslo, 2012.
[52] Ibid.

Also against the creation of the International Energy Agency

In the wake of the 1973 oil crisis the OECD countries felt powerless against the oil-exporting countries (OPEC), who were well organized and coordinated. As customers reliant on being able to buy oil from the OPEC countries, the OECD countries wished to establish closer cooperation aimed at monitoring the energy market. The plan was to examine the possibilities for reducing dependence on imports from the OPEC countries and forming a kind of reverse pole to the OPEC cooperation. The idea again came from the US Minister of Foreign Affairs, then Henry Kissinger. Kissinger proposed using the same arena as George C. Marshall, his predecessor after the war, i.e. Château de la Muette in Paris. The new organization was to use the same secretariat model and headquarters as the OECD. During that very period Norway had struck oil and started exporting oil to its allies and key trading partners, the OECD countries, on a grand scale. On the other hand, owing to its small and open economy, Norway was just as vulnerable as the other countries in the OECD region. The quandary was that the Norwegian Treasury would make good money from OPEC exploiting its oil monopoly while the mainland industry had to watch the markets crumble owing to reduced purchasing power and demand on the part of its most important trading partners.

The antagonism between the oil industry and the onshore industry that is one of the great bones of contention today was playing out even back in the 1970s. The government based its reply to the invitation to take part in the newly created IEA on this dual role. Norway again played the UN card. At the invitation of the US government to attend the conference that would later establish the International Energy Agency (IEA), the Norwegian government again replied that energy matters had to be dealt with in a global context,[53] i.e. within the UN system. The Norwegian proposal to anchor the IEA in the UN was rejected by the other countries – just as when the Americans wished to set up an organization for the Marshall Plan there was little support for the Norwegian view of using the UN system. The government's response was

---

[53] K. Frydenlund, *Lille land, hva nå? Refleksjoner om Norges utenrikspolitiske situasjon*, Oslo: Universitetsforlaget, 1982, p. 45.

silence and a wait-and-see approach, right until the OECD ambassador Jens Boyesen managed to successfully negotiate a special agreement that would give Norway access to valuable information and knowledge about policy development and research in the countries importing Norwegian oil and gas. The Minister of Foreign Affairs, Knut Frydenlund, called it "an arrangement that suited the Norwegian temperament very nicely: we could join in without being involved, or vice versa."[54] Fine diplomatic craftsmanship combined with great sympathy from our neighbours once again gave Norway the chance to bet on two horses: to reassure political forces at home about their fear of losing control of their oil resources while at the same time allowing Norway an outward display of solidarity towards its allies and key trading partners. These days few people know that Norway neither satisfies the requirements for membership of the IEA nor is a full member, as with the EU's Single (or Internal) Market: Norway has participation rights but no voting rights. We have, as it says, "a special agreement". The only countries in Europe not currently members of the IEA are Albania, Bulgaria, Iceland, Lithuania, Latvia, Croatia, Romania, Serbia and Hungary.[55]

---

[54] *Ibid.*, p. 47.
[55] IEA's website, agreement of 9 May 2014, on IEA, Paris, see http://www.iea.org/media/aboutus/history/IEP2014.pdf.

CHAPTER 3

From French Liqueur to the EEA

The EU is the most ambitious collaboration project ever embarked upon by independent countries. It came about as the answer to Europe's horrendous conflicts. It continued in order to tackle international crises, and to facilitate economic growth and stability – which, in a sense, Norway had a chance to jointly benefit from.

The 1970s – a world in stagnation

The vigorous economic growth of post-war Europe came to a halt at the start of the 1970s. The oil-producing countries of the Middle East wanted to punish Israel's US-backed Yom Kippur War against Egypt and Syria. By introducing an embargo on the sale of oil to the USA and the Netherlands, the OPEC countries once again turned off their oil taps and ensured that the price of oil quadrupled. This led to more expensive energy production for industry and households. The price level of goods and services increased, fuelling inflation. The Germans, British, French, Dutch and Italians, as well as the Nordic countries, were all hit by the oil shocks of the 1970s.

Currency fluctuations, trade barriers and low economic growth were reminiscent of the dire period between the first and second world wars, when countries were competing to have the lowest-value currency while ratcheting up custom duties to protect their own companies. Back then it created a vicious circle of inflation and economic bedlam, which finally ended in war – a situation to be avoided at all costs. The Germans in particular were afraid of this dangerous development, and German households began hoarding gold bar in their homes. This was the dramatic backdrop for the heads of state of the EC countries at the end of the 1970s. They realized that new initiatives were needed to create both economic growth and stability. The need to refocus presented itself: from forging a foundation for peace to creating conditions for economic growth and increased prosperity. But the kind of cooperation adopted by the EC countries was inadequate for facilitating new economic growth.

During the 1970s American and Japanese companies were outcompeting European industry. American multinationals like IBM, Xerox, Cola, Levi's and McDonald's captured the global market. In California's Silicon Valley hundreds of technology companies laid the foundation for later success, often based on technological development from the American space industry, like Microsoft and Apple. The Japanese miracle, based on export-driven growth, dominated the TV, electronics and white goods market. One important reason for American and Japanese success was their access to large domestic markets, where they grew to be big and competitive before taking over the global market in step with the gradual opening-up of world trade.

In Europe, the situation was different. Apart from some established multinationals, most countries had their own nationally oriented companies focused on their own markets. For over twenty years, therefore, the European Economic Community, or EEC, as it was originally called, had been trying to dismantle the barriers between the markets and increase trade. Instead of each EC country manufacturing the same type of goods, cosily protected by steep trading restrictions, the aim was now to create a larger market with more competition, lower prices and a broader offering for consumers. It was impossible to generate such economies of scale in Europe unless an industry was state-owned and had access to capital when suitable profits failed to materialize.

Great Britain, France and Germany were hard hit by the economic troubles of the 1970s. The British took issue with the Labour Party's social-democratic policies, electing the leader of the Conservative Party, Margaret Thatcher, Prime Minister in 1979. Thatcher set in motion the comprehensive privatization of key companies and services for which the authorities had been responsible: health, care, energy, finance, air and rail transport. A British cultural revolution, so many thought. In addition, she wielded an iron hand over the striking workers in the loss-making coal mines and thus came to be nicknamed "The Iron Lady".

France went the opposite way. After the crisis in the 1970s, for the first time in the Fifth Republic, the French elected a president from the Socialist Party, François Mitterrand, in 1981. Mitterrand followed an entirely different direction: instead of selling out and privatizing in order to raise income for the state, as Thatcher had done, he gave the new government orders for the state to take over strategic industrial enterprises and all 36 banks.[1] This nationalization of large parts of the economy led to enterprises no longer adapting to the economic reality. At the same time, working hours were cut and social support schemes increased. Central government budget spending increased sharply without income following suit. Confidence in the French franc dwindled and interest rates had to be held up in order to curb inflation, which many people claimed was working counter to economic growth.

Germany's economy was struggling too. The mandate for Deutsche Bundesbank, the West German central bank, was to keep the level of prices stable and keep inflation down. The central bank raised the interest rate to prevent inflation. Businesses were forced to pare their expenditure right down because the high interest rate made bank loans and debt generally more expensive to service. Many people went under because they were unable to service their debt. Workers were dismissed, and the state lost tax revenues and had to pay out more in benefits to an ever increasing number of unemployed. Instead of the central bank lowering the interest rate and encouraging increased spending, as is done nowadays, it kept interest levels up not merely to fight inflation but to avoid weakening the currency. A declining currency would be good for industry, but in this instance it was seen as pouring oil on the inflationary bonfire because all imported goods would become much more expensive and fuel the increase in prices further still.

This reminded the Germans of the situation in the 1920s that formed the basis for the outbreak of fascism. Inflation had to be halted, and the authorities tightened the reins in the form of higher interest and tax increases. This contributed to making German industry less competitive and led to mass redundancies in the sector. In five years, from 1970 to 1975, unemployment in West Germany rose from 200,000 to

---

[1]   D. March, *The euro. The politics of the new global currency*, New Haven, Connecticut: Yale University Press, 2009.

more than 1 million.[2] The age of the German miracle appeared to be over. German industry's wide-ranging and influential special-interest organizations worked hard to deploy any means that could protect their own members' interests and improve their general conditions. One effective measure was to maintain national standards, specifications and special arrangements so as to shut out the competitors from neighbours like France.

The economic unrest in Europe added impetus to national initiatives and special arrangements. The question people asked themselves was: What could the countries do together to re-invigorate economic growth?

The Bretton Woods Agreement and American U-turn

Europe's economic growth during the post-war period was driven largely by demand from the USA. Towards the end of the Second World War, through the Bretton Woods Agreement, the USA had promised the 44 participating countries that they would be able to convert American dollars into gold at a fixed rate of 0.35 dollars an ounce (about 30 grams). It was called "the American gold standard". In the USA, however, the expense of the Marshall Plan, the start of the Vietnam War and extensive involvement in the third world resulted in vast amounts of dollars leaving the country. The USA's negative trade balance with Europe was acceptable as long as Europe could be rebuilt after the war. Twenty-five years after the war and successful reconstruction the USA felt that Europe should readjust its monetary value. No one listened, and with the high dollar rate American industry became increasingly more uncompetitive.[3]

On 15 August 1971 President Richard Nixon announced, to great surprise the world over, that the USA could no longer change dollars into gold. From that day on, the USA also introduced 10 percent customs duty on imports of all goods. The event, which has been

---

2   H. Werner Sinn, "The Laggard of Europe", *CES-Info*, Vol. 4, No. 1, fig. 5, p. 5. See http://www.ifo-institut.info/pls/guestci/download/CESifo%20Forum%202003/ CESifo%20Forum%201/2003/Laggard-of-Europe-2003.pdf.

3   D.P. Calleo, *The imperious economy*, Boston, Massachusetts: Harvard University Press, 1982, p. 69.

dubbed the Nixon shock, led to the value of the American dollar falling considerably against the other large currency units like the Japanese yen and the German mark. The duty slowed down the import of foreign goods, while American exports became cheaper after the devaluation. When the Americans no longer guaranteed the currency value with gold, the world lost the basis for the value of every currency. The value of currency floated freely, so that banks and financial institutions spotted their chance to earn big bucks on speculating in the fall of currencies from countries with a weak economy. The British economist Susan Strange called it a "casino economy": competitiveness built up on the basis of economic moderation, low wage growth and budgetary discipline was lost overnight when the financial markets' currency speculation forced countries to devalue. With Nixon's politics, the USA – the Western world's undisputed leader and champion of economic stability and free trade – had left international cooperation high and dry and bolstered the economic crisis in Europe. American protectionism highlighted Europe's vulnerability, which was amplified by the EC countries' dissension.[4]

This period, dubbed "eurosclerosis", constituted the EC's first great economic crisis. It was this economic and political climate in the 1970s that forced the EC countries to rethink: oil crisis, American economic retreat and an escalating Cold War between east and west.

Cassis de Dijon and the start of the EU's Single Market – the last straw, or rather the final drop

In the 1970s German tourists had acquired a taste for the locally produced sweet French blackcurrant liqueur they drank as an aperitif before meals when holidaying in the South of France, either as a "kir" mixed with white wine or as a "kir royal" in champagne. So German shops wanted to sell the liqueur to their customers, something French producers and exporters had only been able to dream of hitherto. It would prove no easy matter.

During year-long negotiations, EC cooperation had gradually managed to eliminate tariff rates in odd areas, but there were still a

---

[4]   *Ibid.*, p. 77.

great many technical trade restrictions in existence. Each country, just like us here in Norway, had its own specifications and requirements for product standards regarding health, safety and the environment. Bureaucratic and administrative obstacles were common, and were not caught by trade agreements to dismantle customs barriers and quotas either. There was one regime that applied to products from the home country, and another for products from neighbouring countries. Many of these detailed requirements were introduced during the interwar period because the authorities wanted to exclude competing goods for the benefit of national industry, business and trade. The Versailles Treaty after the First World War ordered Germany to pay a large war debt to the allies. Germany was entirely dependent on exporting more than it imported in order to raise money to pay its debt to the victors of the First World War. The point of the trade barriers was to shield national enterprises from foreign competition and at the same time give them a competitive edge over their neighbours. The USA wanted to get to grips with these covert trade barriers using the Marshall Plan after the Second World War. In a spirit of liberalism, the Americans thought that increased cooperation on trade and the production of strategic goods would eventually render war impossible.

Within the Coal and Steel Union and the EEC, both of which were based on supranational cooperation with joint decision-making institutions, all decisions were taken consensually, which is to say that everyone had to agree on everything. That is why it took years to arrive at often watered-down compromises amenable to all of the countries. Charles de Gaulle knew how to exploit this and in some cases blocked EC cooperation entirely for months on end by leaving the negotiating table, a tactic called "the empty chair policy" because no decisions could be made without all countries being present. The blackcurrant liqueur, however, was set to transform the EC – and the EU – for ever.

On 22 April 1978, the German food wholesaler Rewe-Zentral AG accused the federal German administration of imposing unduly restrictive national rules for spirits before the EC Court of Justice, the grievance being that the company was denied the right by the German authorities to market the French blackcurrant liqueur Crème de Cassis from Dijon. The ban originated on account of Germany's home-produced liqueur containing 25 percent alcohol and being consumed in small amounts (like shots of Norwegian aquavit and schnapps). The French version of the same liqueur, however, was 10 percent weaker and enjoyed in a generous-sized wine glass together with white wine or in a tall, slender glass with champagne. The German Attorney-General claimed that changing over to the weaker French liqueur would force German consumers to drink more in order to obtain the same alcoholic effect. This would be detrimental to health and lead to an increase in the number of alcoholics in Germany.[5] "Weak liqueur leads to increased consumption", the Attorney-General insisted. The liqueur had to be kept potent and be drunk in small servings. This, according to the German authorities, was a good reason to exclude French liqueur.[6]

In other words, it was the right to maintain national requirements to protect its own industry and jobs that underpinned the West German Public Prosecutor's strategy to defend his country's interests in the EC Court of Justice.

Early on the morning of 20 February 1979 the auditorium of the EC Court of Justice on Avenue Konrad Adenauer in central Luxembourg was packed. The front bench was occupied by the European Commission's lawyer, surrounded by a dozen clerks and assistants. The Commission's lawyer had claimed that West Germany was using health-policy considerations as a pretext to enable it to protect its own liqueur producers. The Commission thought that excluding competitors was a case of out-and-out protectionism and hence a violation of the EC Treaty. Behind the German Attorney-General's representatives, the Federal Monopoly Administration for Spirits and German Business Interests, sat a pack of representatives from European umbrella organizations for wine and liqueur producers.

The President of the EC Court of Justice, Hans Kutscher, slowly read out the judges' conclusion: "the West German state's wish to protect the health of the country's inhabitants from liqueur with a weak alcohol content, because it might lead to increased consumption, cannot be approved," continuing: "On the other hand, all products made legally in an EU country must be able to be sold freely in all the other countries."

---

5   See   http://ec.europa.eu/enterprise/policies/single-market-goods/files/goods/docs/
    mutrec/cassisdijon_en.pdf.

6   See   http://eur-lex.europa.eu/legal-content/EN/TXT/HTML/?isOldUri=true&uri
    =CELEX:61978Cj0120.

Those sitting in the blue leather chairs on the spectators' bench that day knew that the court ruling was potentially capable of assuming great importance for the development of European cooperation. The trade policy and EC law specialists reckoned the court would break with previous practice and establish a new principle for commerce between sovereign countries.

Until the "Cassis de Dijon" judgment, every country had listed some categories of product and negotiated a reduction and discontinuation of various forms of trade barriers. This is the procedure still used by the World Trade Organization (WTO) to this very day. Oddly enough, the WTO bases this policy on all countries having high customs barriers in order to prevent trade and protect their own industry. In the WTO, all trade is basically illegal. During negotiations, representatives from pairs of countries sit on either side of a table and each presents its offer to reduce protectionist duties. When both countries are satisfied with the market access they have secured from each other, a resolution is adopted. An important feature of the WTO negotiations is that an agreement between two countries can be made operative for all 159 of the other countries. This is an extremely laborious and time-consuming process; and the more countries take part, the longer it takes to reach agreement. Because the negotiating format is based on consensus, every single country also has the option of blocking agreements.

This is the exact same situation that arose recently when India suddenly changed its mind during the WTO's last negotiating round, the so-called Doha Round, which has been going on since 2001. Having agreed to the compromise between all 159 countries in December 2013, India changed its mind because it felt the agreement would place restrictions on its ability to protect its own agricultural sector. Without an agreement, the WTO is currently at risk of losing its position as a facilitator of international trade.

The "Cassis de Dijon" ruling's principle of mutual approval of goods rendered the WTO's negotiating format obsolete between EC countries. By turning the problem on its head, it would no longer be up to the countries to agree on what tariff rate to impose on one another's products. Instead all goods would be freely tradable as long as they satisfied the home country's rules concerning health, safety and the environment, just like selling an article from Finnmark to Akershus, or from California to Florida.

In this way, the EC Court of Justice gave the Commission a new tool for circumventing the old procedure, which blocked all previous attempts to unite the EC countries. It was the key to establishing a uniform and united European market which linked the people in every country together by enabling businesses to trade, invest and establish a presence wherever they wished. People would be able to move, work and pursue an education wherever they pleased. It was this tool which previous attempts to interconnect the countries of Europe lacked, such as the Briand Plan for the French Minister of Foreign Affairs, Aristide Briand, in 1929; the Marshall Plan for the US Secretary of State, George C. Marshall, in 1947; or the concept of the European Coal and Steel Union for Robert Schuman in 1950.

The cost of non-cooperation

The "Cassis de Dijon" ruling simultaneously showed how deadlocked the EC countries' governments were in their old-school ideas, and how they clung to the trade-policy tools from the inter-war period. This was tackled by the visionary trade and industry leader and Volvo manager Pehr G. "PG" Gyllenhammar. In 1983, he took the initiative for a comprehensive study of how to make European industry more competitive and create more jobs. Together with colleagues in the 17 largest concerns in Europe, including Norsk Hydro, he proposed concrete measures for both framework conditions and infrastructure to give Europe's trade and industry more of a competitive edge over its trading partners, especially in view of the global competition from large financial players like the USA and Japan. The group called itself the *European Round Table of Industrialists (ERT)* and still exists to this day. One of the many reports from the ERT, "Missing Link", pointed even then to the need for high-speed trains able to link Scandinavia to the countries on the continent.[7]

At this time, the Commission presented a report which, for the first time, put concrete figures on what European trade and industry was

---

[7]   European Roundtable of Industrialists, Highlights, see www.irt.eu.

losing by way of lack of European cooperation. In the report, entitled "The cost of non-Europe", the Commission highlighted specific losses in terms of efficiency, time and money resulting from different national approaches to rules and regulations for industry, trade and the public sector. The Commission thought the EC countries could earn 8 billion euro, or 6 percent of the EC countries' gross national product, by harmonizing regulations. The forecasts for both the Commission and Gyllenhammar would prove to be modest, however, not to say completely wrong. In a report from August 2014 drawn up by Prognos AG, a forecasting institute, on behalf of the Bertelsmann Stiftung (or Foundation), it emerges that the EU countries have achieved massive economic growth and prosperity as a result of the EU's Single Market. In Denmark, the economic growth ascribable to cooperating with the other EU countries during the period 1992 to 2014 stood at 500 euro per annum per inhabitant. In Germany, the gross national product has grown by 37 billion euro a year. All the countries of Northern Europe have enjoyed annual GNP growth of between 180 and 220 billion euro.[8] The closer the countries' cooperation, the greater the economic benefits. That is why Great Britain also comes out lowest.

According to "*Outside and Inside*", Norway's gross national product for the mainland (i.e. without the oil sector) increased by 60 percent during the period 1994 to 2011. The report was unable to establish how much of this increase was due to Norway's participation in the EU's Single Market, but with 81 percent of Norwegian exports going to the EU, Norway is the country with the fourth-largest share of trade with other EU countries.[9] There is thus reason to believe that Norway will be high on the German forecasting institute's list.

The initiative by ERT, the "Cost of non-Europe" report and the new ruling from the EC Court would prove to be important contributions to the Commission's new strategy. Lord Arthur Cockfield, British Commissioner for Internal Market, Tax Law and Customs Union, and

---

[8]   Prognos AB, See http://www.bertelsmann-stiftung.de/cps/rde/xchg/SID-D0420 E8B-4B3968E9/bst_engl/hs.xsl/nachrichten_121808.htm.

[9]   Europautredningen (Norwegian Europe Review), *Utenfor og innenfor ("Outside and Inside")*, Official Norwegian Report (NOU) 2012, 2, fig. 14.8, EEA-landenes handel (eksport pluss import) med andre EEA-land som andel av deres totale utenrikshandel for 2010, Source: Eurostat and SSB.

Jacques Delors, the new French President of the Commission, worked really well together. In 1985, they tabled a white paper, in which they advocated setting up a uniform market from which all barriers to the free movement of goods, services, capital and people were to be removed. Based on the ruling handed down in the "Cassis de Dijon" case, the EC countries were to recognize one another's requirements, not only in terms of products and services but also technical and higher education and work experience. Delors and Cockfield called it the Single European Act. It set out to establish a common Single Market, with no borders between the EC countries, whether in terms of trade in goods and services or companies and individuals being able to invest, work and settle in whichever country they wished, hence the rather ambivalent and slightly confusing concept of "free movement".

In order to gain support for the radical change, the Commission asked the member states' governments to change the decision-making mechanism in the EU's General Affairs Council, on which all the member states' governments have a seat. Jacques Delors wished to introduce a new principle under which decisions were adopted by a two-thirds majority, instead of waiting for all the countries to agree, i.e. unanimity. The biggest countries – Germany, France, Italy and Great Britain – were to be given 29 votes, then fewer and fewer, down to Denmark with 7 votes and little Luxembourg with 4. This way, no single country could block the negotiations, as had frequently happened before. In addition, the European Parliament had codetermination in the main spheres of the Single Market. This reform was revolutionary in European constitutional thinking and practice. In November 2014, this mechanism was altered so that each country gets only one vote on the Council. The majority must consist of 55 percent of the countries and 65 percent of the population.

These sweeping reforms were presented to the heads of state in the form of a treaty amendment, the first since the Treaty of Rome was concluded in 1957. Several countries had to hold referenda in order to be able to endorse such momentous reforms. The Danes were unable to give the European Parliament legal authority because that meant ceding sovereignty in contravention of its constitution. In the referendum on 27 February 1986 the Danes voted in favour of creating the Single Market: 56.2 percent in favour and 43.8 percent against, with more

than a 75 percent turnout. Ireland also said yes in its referendum, with
no less than 69 percent voting in favour. The new treaty was adopted
and signed on 17 February 1986, and after just 18 months it had been
ratified and came into force. The new decision-making model made
it possible for the EC countries to pass some 90 percent of the 300
or so proposals in Lord Cockfield's white paper by 1992. The white
paper also proposed extensive projects for cooperation on research,
development and innovation in all areas of society in addition to
country-specific programmes for culture, transport, education, energy
and the environment. In parallel with the Single European Act, Delors
set in train cooperation to remove the border crossing points between
EC countries. In the small town of Schengen in Luxembourg the five
EC countries of Belgium, the Netherlands, Luxembourg, France and
West Germany agreed to remove one another's frontier areas and set
up joint external passport control points instead. At the same time, the
countries established a new cooperation between police and customs
authorities. Until that moment, exchanging information and citing
a reason to send emergency services into one another's countries was
entirely out of the question.

What about EFTA?

Just one not inconsiderable problem now remained: Europe was
divided into two owing to the Cold War. Ever since the Second World
War the Moscow regime had taken advantage of every occasion to
prevent European cooperation because it regarded it as a threat to its own
position. At that time, the regime was still coercing half of Europe into
living under political dictatorship and economic misery, just to hang
onto power and disunite any move towards European reconciliation.
Those countries that did manage to usher in democratic reforms by their
laborious political efforts were subjected to coups or brutally invaded, as
with Prague in 1948, East Berlin in 1953, Hungary in 1956 and Poland
in 1981. Ever since the inter-war period Norway had wished to play
the role of bridge-builder between the superpowers. Norway had voted
no to membership of the EC in autumn 1972. Finland and Austria
were obliged to keep out of alliances that might appear threatening to
the Soviet Union, while Sweden and Switzerland wished to maintain

the neutrality which had served them so very well economically during the Second World War. Iceland's interests were confined to selling fish, which at that time accounted for the largest single share of its gross national product. Delors' challenge was that the six EFTA countries were the EC's most important trading partners of all and the key to the Single Market being able to succeed in generating renewed economic growth and increasing prosperity in Western Europe.

Norwegian indifference and shock

The reforms that Jacques Delors' Commission continuously introduced at the beginning of the 1980s would change the EC cooperation from an anonymous and technically oriented organization to a major driving force for economic and political reform and cooperation in Europe. In Norway, it had begun to dawn on the government and the majority of the civil service, albeit ever so gradually, what was brewing.

At first the government viewed the reform proposals in the EC with a healthy portion of distrust and doubt.[10] In light of all the conflicts between the EC countries and the pronounced sluggishness that had dominated negotiations between countries with extremely different cultures, language and temperament, the idea of establishing a large domestic market seemed virtually utopian. The economic problems called for the opposite solution after all: more trade barriers and preferential treatment for domestic industry. The Norwegian response was reminiscent of the attitude to the EC cooperation's initiative a little more than 30 years previously regarding the Coal and Steel Union. The Ministry of Foreign Affairs' considered opinion at that time was that the six countries would neither agree nor manage to ratify (adopt) the agreement in the countries' national assemblies. Certain key people in officialdom, however, were close to the EC's negotiations in Brussels. They recorded the new changes in political outlook and the serious commitment to them. These were competent professionals who were sending home good reports and analyses, but politicians able to convey the message to a wider public they were not.

---

[10] Conversation with Norwegian diplomats.

During the campaigns for the 1961 and 1965 general elections, Prime Minister Gerhardsen requested that the issue of Norwegian affiliation with the EC be kept secret.[11] The same applied to the trendsetting parties at the forefront of the parliamentary elections in 1985 and 1989.[12] They did not want any debate on membership of the EC so hot on the heels of the agonizing 1972 referendum.

Follow-up by the government

The 1987 white paper on "Norway, the EC and European cooperation" appeared two years after the presentation of Jacques Delors' white paper and the launch of the EC's Single Market. The white paper gives a good description of the broad-ranging reforms outlined by the Commission, and warns in clear terms that the EC cooperation is in the process of changing. But instead of portraying it as the beginning of a radical, whirlwind development, the paper gives a minimalist account that just talks about trade, industrial goods, technical standards and competition policy. The political part that deals with follow-up by the Norwegians is scanty. The gist of it is to set up an interdepartmental working party, with representatives of labour and business interests, among others, tasked with the following: "The point is to both obtain information and convey it to all the ministries and bodies concerned and, not least, to make the necessary all-round assessment."[13]

It is a very spartan response. Despite the radical changes to the EC countries' cooperation, the government saw no reason to change Norway's existing affiliation. They were simply supposed to emphasize the flow of information. One practical measure taken to consolidate that information was the government's announcement that it was going to set up a diplomatic station of its own to deal with EC affairs. This, perhaps, is the source of the reason for the government's lack of insight into and commitment to the European integration process: Norway

---

[11]   Ch. Ingebritsen, *The Nordic States and European Unity*, Ithaca, New York: Cornell University, 1998, p. 125.

[12]   Official Norwegian Report (NOU) 2012: *Utenfor og innenfor*, 24.3 EEA-prosessen 1987-1994.

[13]   Norwegian white paper (St.meld.) No. 61 (1986-1987) *Norge, EF og europeisk samarbeid*, 22 May 1987, p. 34.

had next to no diplomatic contact with the EC up to 1987, five years after the Commission started to establish the Single Market. It is no wonder Norway started to lag behind even back then.

The paper did not outline any visions or alternative directions as to what the change in the EC might eventually mean for the continued development of Europe. The reason for the extremely cautious approach was that the government wanted for all the world to avoid the paper leading to a new debate on membership.[14]

Lack of political interest

Looking back at this era, there were not many Norwegian politicians who were genuinely concerned with Norway's role in Europe. Clearly the most prominent was the Minister of Foreign Affairs in the Brundtland governments, the diplomat Knut Frydenlund. With his tragic and sudden death from the aftermath of a stroke at Fornebu Airport in 1987 came the extinction of the one politician Norway had who could communicate foreign policy with authority in a down-to-earth and disarming manner. At the Ministry of Foreign Affairs there were several senior officials with similar knowledge, but none with the same voice inwardly in the Labour Party or outwardly in reaching the people.[15] Frydenlund's death contributed to the influential political department of the Ministry of Foreign Affairs never really putting its heart and soul into pitching EC matters high on the government's or the *Storting*'s political agenda. It was also to blame for the government failing to adequately take to heart developments in Central and Eastern Europe, which at that time was disintegrating. Nor did the government see the other EFTA countries' taking brisk strides towards EC membership. When Austria applied for membership of the EC as early as July 1989, it provoked mirth in the corridors of the Norwegian Ministry of Foreign Affairs.[16] The gravity only started to sink in two years later when Sweden submitted its application in July 1991, followed by Finland

---

[14] *Ibid.*

[15] Conversations with top Norwegian diplomats like the late Arne Arnesen, for whom I worked at the embassy in Beijing.

[16] Conversations with Norwegian diplomats.

seven months later. As so many times before, the Ministry of Foreign Affairs failed to take the signals given by our allies in Europe seriously, and that was instrumental in Norway not handing in its application for membership until December 1992. Preparations for a national debate on Europe got off the ground correspondingly late. The Austrians were given five years, the Swedes three and the Finns two and a half. In Norway, where the resistance was greatest, the government might have seemed to be trying desperately to hold back the historical development of Europe; or, as in Hambro, Lie and Lange's day, denying the existence of Europe.

Gro Harlem Brundtland had both the aptitudes, the appreciation and the opportunities to bump the European question up the political agenda, but her principal concern was the UN and environmental policy in connection with the release of the UN report "Our Common Future". The report tied up considerable human key resources and a good deal of time in the Prime Minister's office and at the Ministries of Foreign Affairs and the Environment. Her personal contact with Jacques Delors was of great importance, and senior officials at the Ministry of Foreign Affairs' Commercial Department would often work directly with the Prime Minister's office on matters related to the EC.[17]

Johan Jørgen Holst (also Labour) was a towering political figure in foreign affairs too, but he concentrated primarily on defence cooperation and the Middle East conflict. The same went for Thorvald Stoltenberg, who in many ways was a genuine European, but became vigorously engaged in global missions as the UN High Commissioner for Refugees and later as a peace broker in the Balkans. That would take him away from Norwegian politics the year before the referendum in 1994.

Frydenlund met the intellectual academics on their home ground but also talked to the people on the streets and the workers on the shop floor, as witnessed by his books *Lille land, hva nå?* and *En bedre organisert verden* ["Little Country, What now?" and "A Better Organized World"]. Kaci Kullmann Five from the Conservative Party of Norway (Right) made a sterling effort to come across as a European but entered national politics too late and disappeared too early to be able to take on a role of Frydenlund's dimensions. It is regrettable that the Ministry of

---

[17]   *Ibid.*

Foreign Affairs has not come to grips with the lack of knowledge about Europe from which Norway suffered. The ARENA research programme at the Centre for European Studies at the University of Oslo is a valiant exception, but its publications and work are extremely academic and barely accessible to most people. Quite simply, the programme makes European politics as dull as dishwater; and if anything it is living proof that Europe is something rather remote and rarefied which only people with a doctorate can relate to. It is surely a historical error that neither the Ministry of Foreign Affairs, the *Storting* nor any Norwegian universities have set up a foundation or scholarship scheme in the name of Knut Frydenlund.

Otherwise, the political landscape in Norway was dominated by the niche Socialist Left Party (SV), the Centre Party (Sp) and the Christian Democrats (KrF), all of whom were concerned with safeguarding their 4-5 percent core voters and getting political mileage out of creating a bogeyman from the capital forces, the EC agricultural and alcohol policy of the time.

Slowly but surely, the government and the civil service gradually realized that Jacques Delors' white paper on the creation of the Single Market would mean a far-reaching change in the EC countries' relationship with Norway and the other EFTA countries. The EC countries would be under legal orders to regard all products, services and investments as their own, i.e. as one big domestic market, while the EFTA countries would be dependent on the old trade agreement from 1973, with its lists of categories of individual products and the exchange of letters between ministers in different countries, as was customary at the time. Every single EFTA country had its own individual agreement with the EC, which meant that updating the agreements would be extremely time-consuming. Norway also realized that it would not have time to complete negotiations to review an area of the trade agreement before new EC reforms rendered them irrelevant.

In addition, the government viewed the fact that Norway's agreements did not cover the new areas of cooperation in the EC with some trepidation. Trading in services, access to one another's public-bidding rounds, protection of investments and the possibility of working, living, training and retiring were altogether inconceivable areas of cooperation in 1973, when the trade agreement was signed. A number of new areas of cooperation like research and development, the environment, education,[18] culture and energy were not covered by the trade agreement either.

From 1986 to 1992 the EC countries negotiated and adopted just over 300 directives and regulations in order to realize Delors' project on the Single Market. All countries were supposed to readjust to the new cooperation. In the process, a spate of trade conflicts arose between the EC and Norway in areas of great importance to Norwegian industry, economy and jobs. The reason was that when the markets in the EC countries were amalgamated, it led to large-scale changes in the form of mergers and closures within the EC countries' business communities. Industry's interest organizations in the EC could not just sit back and watch Norway and other countries carry on production and exports in a way that knocked the stuffing out of their own markets. The Commission therefore asked for trade-policy measures to be introduced in a number of areas.

Trade sanctions against Norway

Without regional cooperation, there is always the risk of falling victim to trade-policy measures and sanctions. It is the World Trade Organization (WTO) that controls the regulations governing these sanctions, usually in the form of antidumping initiatives. When a country's industry can demonstrate lost earnings due to competitors from another country selling the same goods for less than the cost of producing them, a special tariff rate can be introduced to offset the difference in price.

The oil crisis had brought about an economic recession, and the demand for metals slumped on the largest markets of the USA and Japan, leading to overproduction of steel, among other things. Within the Coal and Steel Union the countries agreed to share production amongst themselves. The EC countries stood shoulder to shoulder by distributing the reduction among themselves in such a way that no one country would suffer more than others. The Commission demanded

---

[18]   K. Almestad, *Frihandelsavtalen av 1973. Et alternativ for Norge?* Oslo: The European Movement, 2012, p. 10.

that Norway shoulder its share of the burden; and following a proposal at the EC, therefore, Norwegian industry was forced to both reduce its exports and adjust its steel prices to the EC countries. These measures also resulted in wide-scale and costly inspections and reporting for the companies.

The same happened to the electrometallurgical industry. In other areas like aluminium, the Commission instigated extensive investigations but shelved the case after a year because it considered that the low prices benefited its own industry. However, Norwegian producers of ferro silicon and carbon silicide had to change their price level by agreement with the Commission right from 1983 until the EEA Agreement entered into force in 1994.[19] In 1993 there were 15 Norwegian companies countrywide producing ferro silicon, which made up 55 percent of the European volume and 20 percent globally.[20]

Last but not least, the Commission instigated investigations in 1989 to introduce antidumping measures against the Norwegian fish-farming industry. Following long negotiations, during which the trade brought in its own measures to increase the price level, the Commission shelved the case two years later. The salmon case continued far beyond the 1990s and 2000s with a series of allegations made by breeders from EU countries, leading to minimum-price agreements after long and intense negotiations between Norway and the European Commission. The salmon agreement from 1997 introduced a minimum price on sales of salmon in the EU. The agreement further involved Norwegian breeders having to increase export duty for their own Fish Export Committee (later the Norwegian Seafood Council). Thus Norwegian salmon got slightly more expensive and together with the minimum price it provided some protection for European breeders. The stroke of genius in the agreement was that Norwegian trade and industry could itself spend the money from the increased duties to market its own products. The innovative, and for Norway extremely advantageous agreement, was hammered out over lunch and written down on a serviette[21] by EU Ambassador Einar Bull.

---

[19]   *Ibid.*

[20]   Official Norwegian Report (NOU) 1996, 11, *Forslag til ny minerallov*, Table 5.7.

[21]   T. Foss, "Analyse av Norges avtaler og samarbeid med EU på fiskeriområdet", *Europautredningen* (Norwegian Europe Review), subreport No. 4, 2011, p. 24.

Having to feel constantly subject to the threat of trade policy measures from one's most important market gradually became unbearable for Norwegian industry. Even if agreement was successfully reached in some cases before the Commission imposed fines or other forms of sanctions, the actual process was resource intensive for companies, which were constantly having to answer lengthy surveys about production, prices and market. That took energy and resources away from the companies' core business in addition to racking up bills for lawyers' and lobbyists' fees.

Another area that affected Norwegian trade and industry was the EC's competition regulations, the point of which is to prevent companies consciously collaborating with competitors in order to keep price levels up. Worldwide, cooperation between the oil-producing countries in OPEC is the worst example of this. The OPEC countries meet regularly to agree on the production, sale and hence price level of oil and gas. For other sectors, such collaboration tends to take place during conferences or during meetings at hotels. One example is the directors of the world's largest pharmaceutical companies, who met once a year at the luxurious Dolder Hotel outside Zürich. There they agreed on the price level of important medicines around the world. The same applied to the liner companies that maintained regular shipping routes between all the world's continents. They were gradually granted exemption from the EU's competition regulations because such large investments were at stake that they had to be given the chance to maintain a certain price level in order to meet their costs.

Large Norwegian companies like Borregaard and Statoil were targeted and fined by the Commission because they had been collaborating illegally with their competitors. To the Norwegian government's great surprise, the cartel cases involving Norwegian companies were not heard on the Mixed Committee between Norway and the EC, as suggested by the 1973 trade agreement. Instead the Commission dealt with the cases in its own fora, where Norway was not represented.[22] This is an altogether natural consequence of our not having access to our trading partners' institutions. It meant that the institutions in our agreements

---

[22] K. Almestad, *Frihandelsavtalen av 1973, Et alternativ for Norge*, Oslo: The European Movement, February 2012, p. 10.

and the Norwegian authorities were blatantly ignored whenever important conflicts arose to threaten the EC countries' industry.

The greatest challenge for Norway, however, would prove to be that the EC cooperation's Single Market introduced equal rights vis-à-vis all the countries' authorities, police and courts for people (individuals) and companies. Norwegian students avail themselves of this right when they pay the same study fees at a Dutch university as the Dutch themselves. The same happens when Telenor establishes a presence or buys up a company in Denmark, and when Norwegian pensioners in Spain gain entitlement to treatment at Spanish hospitals; or when a rich businessman like Kjell Inge Røkke complains about having to pay steep landing charges at the airfield in Nice because the French aviation authorities do not know that planes from Norway must be treated on an equal footing with aircraft registered in EU countries.

The free trade agreement from 1973 which Norway had with the EC said nothing about these rights because the agreement only covered customary trade in industrial goods. In 1973 there was no appetite to give people and companies the option of anything other than buying and selling goods and services produced at home in their own country. The new opportunities which the EC countries were in the process of giving one another were of an entirely different dimension and fell outside the scope of the agreement Norway had. If EC cooperation succeeded in establishing the Single Market, it would mean that citizens from Norway and the other EFTA countries would be subject to discrimination and differential treatment as compared with citizens in EC countries in a great many areas.[23] The staff at the Norwegian Ministry of Foreign Affairs realized with some anxiety that the agreement Norway had with the EC had simply become obsolete: the agreement failed to encapsulate developments in the EC and was incapable of tackling the challenges faced by European economies.

If Norway was to take part in Jacques Delors' new project, utterly innovative thinking was called for. The ideas and views Norway had championed during the creation of the OEEC, the Nordic Council and EFTA, about opposing all forms of supranational cooperation, would become difficult, if not impossible, to uphold.

---

[23] *Ibid.*, p. 12.

The process that began with the "Cassis de Dijon" ruling in 1979 and continued with the Commission's early development of the idea of a European Single Market at the beginning of the 1980s, was completed in 1986. Three years later the heads of state from the EFTA and the EC countries met for the first time to discuss how the EFTA countries could join in the pioneering project started by the EC. For ten years the EC countries' authorities, industries and business communities had been preparing for the opening of the Single Market. If Norway were to join now, it would take an unparalleled herculean effort on the part of the Norwegian administrative authorities. For 40 years Norway had succeeded in keeping the OEEC, EFTA and the Nordic Council out of any supranational cooperation. If Norway took part in the EC's Single Market, all this would be jeopardized. The Norwegian government had a big problem on its hands, therefore: the creation of the EC's Single Market had put the kaibosh on its foreign-policy model.

During the Willoch government from 1981 to 1985 the Minister of Trade, Arne Skauge, saw what was afoot. He took the initiative to bring the EC and the EFTA countries together to discuss developments in the EC. At the meeting in Luxembourg in 1984 the parties agreed to establish negotiations in the EC's new fields of cooperation. Four years later no fewer than 32 negotiating parties had been set up. Little by little, however, it dawned on the negotiators that they were unable to keep pace with developments in the EC; for while the EC countries were introducing common legislation to remove trade barriers based on the "Cassis de Dijon" principle, each of the EFTA countries had its own list of products and national schemes. The Norwegian negotiators demanded market access in areas where Norwegian trade and industry was asserting its presence while spinning out negotiations in areas with great trade obstacles that were protecting Norwegian interests against the competition from neighbouring countries, with no appreciation for what was happening. The mindset and the tactics from the Marshall Plan negotiations, assessment of the country's participation in the European Coal and Steel Union, and the Nordic Customs Union had not changed. Delors and the representatives from many EC countries saw this and told Norway in no uncertain terms that she had to stop practising this form of cherrypicking[24] – just enjoying the benefits while the other countries had to pick up the rest. Norway still wished to play the part of a sort of freeloader sponging off Europe.

The EEA is born

The EFTA countries were unquestionably the EC's most important trading partners. It was in the EC countries' and Commission President Jacques Delors' interest to find a way of including EFTA in the Single Market. Nor did the EC wish to give the appearance of "fortress Europe", built to keep out trade with other countries; so it had been agreed that the EFTA countries would continually evaluate the EC's decisions. The negotiations with each individual EFTA country, which always lagged behind owing to the rapid developments in the EC, proved unmanageable for the Commission and the EC's member states. Furthermore, the Commission had to spend a great deal of time whenever an area came up that Norway and the other EFTA countries did not want. This gave rise to the question of how the EC cooperation, headed by Jacques Delors, could get the EFTA countries to change their attitude towards European cooperation. That forced the Commission to think along entirely new lines.

One cold winter's morning between Christmas and New Year's Eve in 1988, Jacques Delors' Chief of Staff, Pascal Lamy, took a red-eye flight from Brussels and landed at the airport in Oslo, which was then at Fornebu in Bærum. In the taxi driving in along Sjølystveien he saw the lovely morning sun rise over the surface of the sea like a blinding light between the white snow and the blue sky. In his brown leather suitcase, he had the draft of a speech he had been working on for some time. Delors had asked Lamy to look at how the EFTA countries could take part in the new Single Market without becoming a member of the EC. Together with the legal experts from the Commission's legal department, Lamy had arrived at a proposal setting out that the EFTA countries would be allowed to take part in the decision-making fora

---

[24] Willy De Clercq, European Commissioner for External Relations and Trade's statement on the ministerial meeting between the EC and the EFTA countries in Interlaken, May 1987.

that dealt with internal-market legislation. In practice that would mean Norway being allowed to send representatives to the EC's decision-making bodies, both the Commission and the Council of Ministers. The EC Commission would monitor identical introduction and enforcement by all countries of the EC and EFTA. If conflicts arose, these were to be settled at a joint court. The point was to give the EFTA countries the option to take part in the continuous development of laws and rules for the Single Market. In addition, they were to introduce the same regulations governing competition and state subsidies so that no company could abuse its position if it got too big. Nor would the state be able to subsidize a cornerstone company so as to give it advantages over competitors in the other countries.

Having the EFTA countries abide by the same rules for the new market would save all the arduous negotiations about market access in every product area with each country. All internal-market regulations would thus be introduced perfectly equally and at the same time in both EC and EFTA countries.

The fishing and agricultural sectors would be kept out. Previous dialogue between the EC and EFTA had shown that it would be too taxing to reach agreement in these areas.

The concept was called "the European space". The idea was simple yet brilliant. Delors kept his cards close to his chest, having consulted only Gro Harlem Brundtland and their fellow party member, Austrian Prime Minister Bruno Kreisky, about the details of the new project. Lamy would now present the plan to Prime Minister Brundtland's chief of staff Eldrid Nordbø and State Secretary Morten Wetland. His English was like a reprise of Peter Sellers' role as Inspector Clouseau in *The Pink Panther:* his vocabulary was exemplary, but his accent was rather thick.

Once the meeting with the Commission President's head of cabinet at the Prime Minister's office was over, Nordbø and Wetland sat looking at each other. The moment had come when Norway had to take a stance on the EC's revolutionary changes. It was clear to them that three essential challenges lay ahead: Firstly, the EFTA countries could no longer negotiate singlehandedly with the EC but had to agree to speak with one voice. They had never come even close to doing that, owing to the conflicts between the countries over fish, industry and finance. Secondly, Delors' vision of a great European space based on the

EC's rules would threaten the traditional Norwegian attitude towards participating in supranational cooperation and national case law. Thirdly, the remit was enormous. Negotiations would involve the whole of the Norwegian administrative machinery: all ministries, all directorates and other underlying departments and services. That process had to be piloted from the Prime Minister's office, not from the Ministry of Foreign Affairs. In that case the Prime Minister's office would need reinforcements, preferably by way of a French-speaking person who could communicate well with Delors' head of cabinet. After some weeks of searching, Eldrid Nordbø called in a young French-speaking man with a superb reputation from the BI project "Scenario 2000". This was how Jonas Gahr Støre arrived at the centre of power in Norway: his task was to monitor and coordinate the EEA negotiations between all ministries and the EC.

Norway's reply

During the plenary meeting of the European Parliament on 17 January 1989 Jacques Delors presented the idea of a European economic space. The EC countries were already well underway setting up the new and revolutionary Single Market. He now welcomed the EFTA countries in so that they could take part from the first day, i.e. 1 January 1993. That then left little time to agree how the EFTA countries could copy the EC's rules and remain in the Single Market from day one. In his speech Delors made no bones about the fact that the EFTA countries had to radically change their form of cooperation and consent to address the EC with one voice.

In reality, the EC Jacques Delors presented to Norway in 1989 was from the Europe of the 1980s. Once again, we were slow off the mark.

In this way the European economic "space", later to become the European Economic Area, better known as the EEA, was conceived and presented by the EC Commission. Delors' speech, which from a historical perspective laid the foundation for Norway's participation in the EU's Single Market, received lamentably little attention in Norway. In a leader in *Aftenposten*, three days before Delors' speech in Strasbourg, the paper criticized Prime Minister Brundtland's lack of vision in the EC matter, yet at the same time sympathized with the government's wish to avoid a new EC battle "on a par with what we experienced in 1972".[25] *Aftenposten's* correspondent Per Nordrum highlighted the question of how Norway's government would respond to the invitation from Delors. Three weeks later he reported that *Storting* MPs Kaci Kullmann Five and Jan Petersen were calling for a Norwegian response to Delors' lead.[26] They thought the Labour government's reasoning about "not spending resources on anything but adapting to the EC" no longer held water. In practice, it would mean having to wait for the EU countries to agree in order to find a way of affiliating Norway.

EFTA drama

Prime Minister Brundtland took the swift initiative of calling a meeting with her prime ministerial colleagues in the other five EFTA countries with a view to replying to Delors' invitation. On 28 March they met at the Holmenkollen Park Hotel in Oslo. The highly contentious issue was whether the EFTA countries could introduce the musketeer principle of "One for all and all for one"; that is to say, agree on common negotiating positions and speak with one voice in dealings with the EU countries. That issue would eventually become fisheries. Iceland was unable to agree to take part in collective negotiations unless the EFTA partners agreed among themselves on the free trading of fish. If the EFTA countries could not trade freely in fish, they could not expect the EC countries to accept the same. Of the EFTA countries, it was the Swiss who put up the toughest resistance. From Lakes Geneva, Neuchatel, Maggiore and Constance, some 3,000 tonnes of freshwater fish were caught a year, mostly salmon and trout, occupying 292 fishermen full-time in 1987.[27] These piddling little hauls (by way of comparison, Iceland was catching 1.6 million tonnes of freshwater fish a year)[28] would be priced out of the market if Switzerland opened up to the free importation of fish from Iceland and Norway. Finland and Sweden also wished to protect their fishing interests. For Iceland, it was

---

[25]   Uten visjoner, leading article in *Aftenposten*, Wednesday, 18 January 1989.

[26]   P. Nordrum, *Aftenposten*, 2 February 1989.

[27]   Food and Agriculture Organization of the United Nations (FAO): Inland fisheries of Europe, http://www.fao.org/docrep/009/t0377e/t0377e26.htm.

[28]   Statistics Iceland, European Parliament report, Fisheries in Iceland, Brussels, 2008.

important not to be left standing on its own, negotiating fish with the EC when all the other EFTA countries had had their demands satisfied. Switzerland would not budge and stuck to its guns. It would take many hours into the wee small hours until Sweden's Prime Minister, Ingvar Karlsson, managed to persuade his colleagues that relatively small local interests could not block the historic possibility afforded EFTA to become part of the trendsetting cooperation project in Europe.[29]

Both the EC Commission and EFTA's prime ministers stressed the need for the new agreement to respect the other's decision-making process and sovereignty. This was black on white in the communiqué from EFTA's ministerial meeting in June 1989. The problem was that Delors' speech to the European Parliament clearly indicated intentions to establish a common decision-making body and administration.[30] Few, if any, said anything about the combination of respect for each country's sovereignty and a new, collective decision-making body not making ideal bedfellows. The EU Court of Justice provided clarity on this point when it later established that the EFTA countries could not have access to negotiations between the EC countries. Nor could they have a common court. That meant that the agreement which the parties signed on 2 May 1992 in Oporto, Portugal, looked completely different from the proposal Jacques Delors had presented to the European Parliament three years earlier.

1989, Europe's fateful year

1989 was to prove a fateful year for Europe. From 1979 and throughout the 1980s the Polish workers and their trade union *Solidarnosc* (*Solidarity*) forced through ever more demands that threatened the Soviet-controlled Communist dictatorship in Warsaw. The Soviet economy was stagnating and no longer managing to keep up with the American arms race. The President of the Soviet Union, Mikhail Gorbachev, saw no option but to introduce political and economic reforms based on openness and a market economy. The US

---

[29]   Conversation with Jón Baldvin Hannibalsson, minister of Foreign Affairs of Iceland, form 1988-1995, B. Thorhallsson, *Reformulation of Icelandic foreign policy 1991-2007*, Reykjavik: Hid islenska bokmenntafélag, 2008.

[30]   *EFTA bulletin*, No. 3/1989, p. 17.

President, Ronald Reagan, followed up John. F. Kennedy's speech in Berlin from 1963, shouting that famous sentence during his speech to the Berliners in June 1987: "President Gorbachev: Tear down this wall!" All spring and summer long in 1989, East German citizens swarmed together in Hungary's capital Budapest to seek political asylum at the Austrian Embassy. So great was the crush that the Hungarians finally had to cut open the barbed-wire fencing on the border between Austria and Hungary: the Iron Curtain Churchill had warned of in 1946 had finally been sheared open. On 9 November 1989 East German citizens stormed the wall in Berlin. The whole world held its breath for fear of the borderguards' reaction: Would they open fire on the demonstrators as they had done for 28 years? They pretended nothing had happened. Overnight the wall was hacked to pieces, and one after another, little East German cars drove through the huge barriers, cheered on by West Berliners, their eyes full of tears of joy. Twenty-eight years of incarceration had come to an end. Europe could now be united. And so the basis for the EEA was gone: the EEA was a product of the Cold War. It was supposed to ensure that countries from different parts of the political spectrum were brought closer together economically. Now that the political causes were no longer present, the EEA was not necessary either; and as far back as 1989, three years before the EEA negotiations had finished, Austria applied for membership of the EC. Sweden and Finland followed suit in 1991.

PART 2

EUROPE-BOUND

CHAPTER 4

Vote for What?

In 1994 people were told the EEA was a good alternative to membership of the EU. All the indicators pointed up – in economic, political and sporting terms. Few people had any inkling of how cooperation between countries worked and would develop in practice. For Norway, Europe boiled down to a question of whether it was economically worthwhile, there and then.

Tipping the scales

Jens P. Heyerdahl d.y., one of Norway's foremost captains of industry through the ages, walked over energetically to where I was standing near the barbecue during the power company Statkraft's annual garden party one summer's day in August 2009. Having commented on the excellent food, he still had something else on his chest, I guessed. Two months earlier, somewhat surprisingly, I had been elected leader of the European Movement. I thanked Heyerdahl politely for his congratulations and waited for his personal EU anecdote, for just about any words of congratulation on this presidential position in the European Movement were followed by an intense desire to mollify every individual's personal experience from the controversial referendum in 1994.

Heyerdahl's story was this: He had recently received a warming invitation to dinner from the 1994 No-queen, Anne Enger (formerly Lahnstein). To mark the occasion of the imminent 15-year anniversary of the No-victory, Enger wished to thank Heyerdahl for going out among the media and announcing his clear opposition to Norwegian membership of the EU in the very last week before the referendum. In 1991 the Orkla Group had bought up Nora Industries and consolidated as Norway's largest manufacturer of branded goods in the food sector. When Heyerdahl was the manager of Orkla, he produced impressive results. During the period when he was group managing director in 1979-2001, Orkla's annual turnover increased from NOK 146 million to 45 billion. The high growth yielded an average return of an amazing 24.1% p.a. for its shareholders.[1] High Norwegian customs barriers on imports of staples like jam, pizza, chocolate and mineral water were an effective way of protecting Orkla's products from competition with its neighbours, Denmark and Sweden, as well as the rest of Europe. Membership of the EU would dismantle the tariff wall, so Heyerdahl had obvious economic incentives for saying No. Nowadays, these food products are the very area where we find the greatest price differential between Norway, Sweden and other countries in Europe.

One of the most powerful arguments against opening up domestic markets was the risk of being outcompeted by producers from other countries. Permitting trade with neighbouring countries posed a threat to many important industrial and cornerstone companies in Norway. This fear manifested itself for the Orkla Group in 1994. Heyerdahl Jnr. proudly told me that Enger thought such an important voice in Norwegian industry as he represented had caused many doubters to come down on the No-side, especially one important group:

"You persuaded one strategic social group: *the cab drivers!*" Enger had told him. "The cab drivers" is another expression for the voice of the people, those who often draw quick conclusions, shoot from the hip, and come out with plain-speaking, fresh and logical expressions.

Through the Confederation of Norwegian Enterprise (NHO) and the Norwegian Shipowners' Association, the rest of the business community had actively advocated in favour of EU membership. The Director-General of NHO, Karl Glad, formerly director-general and group managing director of Aker and chairman of the board of several important industrial companies such as Kongsberg Defence Systems and the ironworks Norsk Jernverk, played a central role in mobilizing NHO's policies and sizable economic resources on the Yes-side. The Shipowners' Association also made a splash among the Norwegian public with a large-scale advertising campaign about why EU membership was in the best interests of Norway: the association was against EU policies and wanted to get in to change them from the inside. Naturally enough,

---

[1]   Orkla's 2001 annual report.

Orkla manager Heyerdahl's dissenter role caused a great stir among the media and among most people. Having one of the biggest heads of industry plump for another point of view and swim against the tide was a ready-wrapped gift to the No-side.

"You were the weight that tipped the scales", Enger had told him, and that had earned him an invitation to dinner. Heyerdahl was looking forward to that dinner.

Anne Enger was right. There was actually very little to it. Although the result of the referendum on 28 November 1994 ended with 52.2 percent to the No-side and 47.8 to the Yes-side, it all came down to precisely 124,110 votes. Had 62,000 votes inched over to the Yes-camp, the outcome would have been very different. It was a small margin for a country of 4.3 million inhabitants and 3.2 million qualified voters.[2]

Nuts and bolts

A widespread view in Norway is that the EEA Agreement mostly contains directives and regulations of a technical nature or, as Trond Giske likes to put it: the EEA is all about nuts and bolts. That is to say, the technical standards introduced are important to industry, but of little importance to politics. The following examples illustrate Norway's take on two EU initiatives at a technical and political level.

1. CO_2 storage

Åslaug Haga from the Centre Party experienced Norwegian lobbying potential in practice when her government wished to contribute to new EU regulations. During her time as oil and energy minister the EU countries negotiated a directive of great importance to Norway. The directive was supposed to lay down how the authorities permit petroleum companies to store CO_2 underground, or in "geological formations" as they say in the jargon.

The starting point was that the government had attached great prestige to developing a technology capable of capturing and storing CO_2 from energy production from fossil sources like coal, oil and gas. This

---

[2]   SSB, 1994 referendum on Norwegian membership of the EU, Table 1.

is known as "carbon capture and storage" (CCS). Prime Minister Jens Stoltenberg called the development of this technology Norway's "moon landing" in his 2007 New Year's speech. It is because he thought CCS would be able to contribute just as much to the world's technological development as the USA's moon landing did up to 1969. The EU's undertaking to prepare the way for regulatory instruments to add impetus to the development of CCS technology was therefore received with great enthusiasm by the government. As the Commission's proposal for a directive on CO_2 storage was being formulated, the Norwegian experts from the Ministry of Petroleum and Energy, the Ministry of the Environment and the Environment Agency had been actively involved in the work, as stipulated by the EEA Agreement. The draft directive now had to be published and sent across for consideration and adoption by the EU's decision-making body, the Council of Ministers and the European Parliament. On 23 January 2008, the Commission tabled a draft of the directive, presented in a white paper, or communication, to the EU's Council of Ministers and the European Parliament, as they say in Brussels. But time was running out: in practice, the member states and the European Parliament had just ten months to debate, negotiate and adopt the directives.

The decision-making bodies of the EU usually take their time, often too much time, to negotiate agreement between all the countries on the Council of Ministers and representatives of the European Parliament. From the day, the Commission presents the draft directive till both decision-making bodies reach agreement, it can certainly take two or three years, sometimes even longer. This time it was different: At the EU summit meeting in March 2007 the German Chancellor Angela Merkel had gained support for an ambitious energy and climate policy, aka the 2020 Package, in which the EU countries agreed to reduce greenhouse gas emissions by 20 percent by the year 2020. In order to achieve those targets, the EU would introduce directives on trading emission quotas, energy savings, increasing the uptake of renewable energy like solar and wind power, and last but not least a new set of regulations to permit CO_2 storage. The directives, called the Energy and Climate Package, were to be adopted ahead of the UN's climate-negotiating meeting in Copenhagen in December 2009. Angela Merkel and the other heads of state wanted the EU countries to lead the way for other countries by adopting legally binding obligations well in advance of the Copenhagen summit. If they could get countries like the USA and China on side, they were willing to increase emission cuts from 20 to 30 percent.

Norway has longstanding experience of storing millions of tonnes of CO_2 under the seabed. Statoil has been doing it at the Sleipner Field in the North Sea since 1996. After Norway introduced a CO_2 tax in 1991, Statoil worked out that it was considerably cheaper to re-inject the greenhouse gas down to where the gas was first obtained than to discharge it into the atmosphere. The storage facility in the geological formations is located approximately 2,000 metres under the seabed. The Norwegian experience was unique because it was the first time such large quantities of CO_2 had been stored. No EU country could boast of the same track record.

Paradoxically, Norway had not put in place regulations of its own to grant the petroleum companies permission to inject CO_2 back underground. Such regulations would include risk management, division of responsibilities and other permits of a technical nature. Instead, the Oil Directorate used existing frameworks to extract oil and gas. Since the EU would be negotiating its own CO_2 storage regulation, this was a unique opportunity for Norway to share our experience with the EU countries and ensure that the body of regulations was brought into line with Norwegian petroleum legislation.

CO_2 storage was something completely new to the vast majority of EU countries. Their scepticism was immense and wide-ranging in Germany, Greece, Denmark and Sweden. Conversely, Great Britain, Romania, the Netherlands and France were quite familiar with the technology. They wanted the Norwegians to attend the meetings between the EU's member states on the Council of Ministers in order to explain what it was all about to the sceptical countries. Under the EEA Agreement, however, Norway's representatives are excluded from attending the negotiations on the Council of Ministers and at the European Parliament.

Åslaug Haga came to Brussels and delivered the keynote presentation at a large hearing in the European Parliament in March 2008. There she saw how significant the EU's negotiations were for Norway. She therefore took the unusual step of asking her Ministry to send a informal enquiry over to the Commission to ask whether Norway might be allowed to take part in the Council of Ministers' negotiations, i.e. the decision-making process which her party has no desire for Norway to participate in. Haga, in other words, side-lined the whole of the Centre Party's and the Soria Moria Declaration and asked whether her own ministry might be allowed to join in with the EU.

The request from the Norwegian oil and energy minister was turned down by the Commission. The reason was that the Commission was obliged to observe the EEA Agreement forbidding Norwegian participation in negotiations between EU member states. Norway has neither the right nor the option to take part in the EU's Council of Ministers. The EU countries adopted the directive towards the end of 2008. They did not manage to solve the problems relating to who should bear financial responsibility for the underground CO_2 store. Norway was the only country in the world to have any hands-on experience of these very topics. Today the unresolved issues relating to financial responsibility are held up as one of the most important reasons for the lack of success in building CCS demonstration plants in Europe.

2. Norwegian input at political level

In a booklet published by the Norwegian Ministry of Foreign Affairs in September 1994, about eight months before the referendum, one of the first pages says that "The EEA gives us opportunities to influence regulations [...] but not the right to take part in the EU's decision-making process". It goes on to say that "[w]hen new EEA rules have to be drawn up, there will be ongoing dialogue and consultation between EFTA and the EC pillar up to the point of their adoption"; and "this is important to ensure that the EFTA countries' interests are protected".[3] One of the key lobbying fora was supposed to be the EEA Council, where foreign ministers from the EFTA countries meet their colleagues from the EU countries. It wasn't like that. What follows is the story of a Minister of Foreign Affairs, Knut Vollebæk, who was supposed to assert Norwegian defence and foreign-policy interests to the best of his ability at a meeting with his EU colleagues.

---

[3]   Informasjon om EEA-avtalen, Norwegian Government's Information Committee on European Affairs, January 1994, p. 39.

Participation in EU defence and foreign policy

Knut Vollebæk was starting to grow quite weary as he sat on the red chairs outside the meeting room at the EU's Council of Ministers for the fifth hour in a row. It's the large pink marble building called after the Belgian philosopher Justus Lipsus, located near the Schuman roundabout in the middle of the EU's headquarters. All the EU countries' governments meet there. The finance and foreign ministers meet every month. The other ministerial positions, such as transport, trade and the environment, only meet four times a year. In the meeting room behind closed doors Vollebæk's colleagues from the EU countries sat engrossed in discussions. It was December 1999, and the foreign ministers of Iceland, Liechtenstein and Norway were sitting waiting to join the EEA Council meeting that was meant to be the forum for dialogue between the EU countries and the EFTA countries' foreign ministers, as they met every spring and autumn.

Since 1994 the EU foreign ministers' interest and participation in the EEA meeting had been on the decline. As usual the meeting with Norway, Iceland and Liechtenstein had taken place on day two of the General Affairs Council, when all the EU countries' foreign ministers meet. By that time the vast majority of cabinet ministers had already returned to their capitals, and only the ambassadors or their deputies were left. Some countries even send their newly-qualified visiting trainees when meetings are of minimal interest. This time the Norwegian chairmanship, and the EFTA secretariat, had been pressing our Finnish neighbours, who had presidency of the EU, to hold the meeting with the EFTA countries on the day when all the ministers were present. Acknowledging Norway as an important dialogue partner intrinsically signalled both prestige and recognition on the part of the EU.

While Vollebæk and his colleagues from Iceland and Liechtenstein waited in the corridor outside the great meeting hall at the Council of Ministers, the EU's foreign ministers sat in tricky discussions. They were supposed to reach agreement on a new chapter in EU defence and safety policy. The plan was for the EU's heads of state to meet in Helsinki a fortnight later and adopt an agreement on how the EU countries, in- and outside of NATO, were to formulate a common European safety and defence policy. The ambitions and the political line had already been laid down, but the details of how to coordinate the use of military troops in conflict situations in the EU's proximity zones were left outstanding, together with others. The result was that the EU would have a fully operational safety and defence policy by 2003, with a European response force of up to 60,000 soldiers, amongst other things.

For the Bondevik I government, in which Knut Vollebæk was Minister of Foreign Affairs, the discussions were extremely relevant and important. Norway had hitherto taken a very sceptical view of the EU's plans for closer cooperation on defence and security.

The outlook and the objective were to avoid any development that might contribute to a weakening of NATO's role. The government was banking on Great Britain's close and privileged relationship with the USA providing a guarantee against opting for closer and more binding cooperation on defence and security policy with its EU partners.

Since the EU countries' early discussions on defence cooperation at the beginning of the 1970s, all governments had considered it completely unrealistic that Great Britain would enter into closer, binding and supranational cooperation in this field. As late as 1998, just months before the Anglo-French summit in Saint-Malo at which Tony Blair and Jacques Chirac signed the historic agreement that formed the basis of the EU's new defence cooperation, the government dismissed this possibility in a white paper:[4] "Great Britain was our guarantor against the EU's defence cooperation." The government saw no advantages to such cooperation because "it would turn the EU into a 'defence alliance', which would have an adverse effect on both the EU's enlargement process and its relationship with Russia".[5] This was the same attitude that Minister of Foreign Affairs Lange had had towards the proposals about the new European cooperation tabled at the OEEC in Paris after the war.

What Norway failed to see was that the British wished to compensate for the influence they lost in the EU as a result of not joining the Euro cooperation, because Prime Minister Blair saw a great need to compensate

---

[4]   Norwegian white paper (St.meld.) No. 22 (1997-1998), *Hovedretningslinjer for Forsvarets virksomhet og utvikling i tiden 1999-2002.*

[5]   B.O. Knutsen, "Norge og utviklingen av EUs sikkerhets- og forsvarspolitikk", FFI-Fokus, Oslo: FFI, 2010, p. 3.

for not taking part in the kernel of the economic cooperation by taking command of the defence policy. He then had to agree to France's long-held and emphatic desire to establish a European defence cooperation.

An Anglo-French agreement was therefore signed in Saint-Malo on the Brittany coast on 4 December 1998. The following year the EU was set to adopt a milestone in European defence policy history, with Great Britain in the driver's seat: the foundation for the European Security and Defence Policy (ESDP). The European Security Declaration lay the foundation for the creation of both civilian and military cooperation. The aim was to respond to the new security policy challenges and prevent terrorism, the proliferation of weapons of mass destruction, state collapse and organized crime. Since 2003 the EU forces have taken part in 23 military and civilian operations, 13 of which were still in progress in 2014.[6] Norway has been following this development with interest and a large portion of scepticism. To make up for its non-participation in the political discussion, Norway has taken part in nine of the EU-led operations and is thus the country with the third-greatest degree of involvement of all the EU countries. A Norwegian naval frigate took part in Operation *Atalanta* near the Gulf of Aden off the Horn of Africa in 2008 and 2009. One hundred and fifty Norwegian soldiers are also taking part in the EU's Nordic Battlegroup. Militarily, this group is under Swedish command. The group was on standby in 2008 and 2011. It is due to be mobilized to full readiness again in 2015. Norway will be asked formally when the group is to take part in acts of war. In ongoing strategic discussions about the group's deployment, however, Norway is thrown back on Sweden to convey its views.

Norway wishes to take part in these operations partly because it provides military and political insight into the margins of the EU's political discussions on domestic defence.

For Norway, the defence cooperation initiated by the EU presented considerable challenges but also opportunities. In retrospect, researchers have stressed the importance for Norway of other Nordic countries participating in the EU's defence cooperation. Our Nordic neighbours can act as Norway's "agents" by putting forward Norwegian views and arguments if they happen to coincide with their own. They also

---

[6]   *Ibid.*

act as a valuable listening post for keeping informed about political dialogue and development. Even in a white paper from 2001, however, the government did admit that "consultation schemes, dialogue and involvement in hands-on crisis management operations could only compensate so far for Norway not being part of this ongoing consultation within the ESDP".[7]

On the other hand, emphasis is given to the fact that our Nordic neighbours want to prioritize the EU's defence policy fora at the expense of existing Nordic meeting places. Bjørn Olav Knutsen, one of Norway's foremost researchers into EU defence policy, says: "It will lead to Norway increasingly being left out when Nordic countries coordinate their policy, or at any rate to Norway having to spend more time and energy on being heard, and possibly being heeded."[8] Up to 2010 Norway, together with other NATO countries outside the EU, were allowed to meet the EU countries' presidency at ministerial level. This generally happened over a cup of coffee straight after the meeting between all the EU defence ministers. It provided valuable insight and ensured a continuous flow of information on decisions and the policies being forged by the EU countries.

Once the Lisbon Treaty entered into force, these brief consultations were phased out. Norwegian Minister of Defence Grete Faremo said in 2010: "We are actively working to bring about a new and acceptable scheme. This is important for safeguarding Norwegian interests."[9] But Norway has not managed to establish such a scheme. As of today, there are no political conversations at cabinet minister level between Norway and the EU in this field. That is how far off the radar Norwegian defence policy interests are in present-day Europe. It is an issue that no Norwegian politician has raised. At a technical level Norway participates in the EU's European Defence Agency (EDA) (aka the European Defence Community (EDC)), the objective of which is to strengthen the EU's defences. The EDA is an important forum for developing what is known as smart defence, i.e. research and development of defence

---

[7]   Norwegian white paper (St.meld.) No. 12 (2000-2001) *Om Norge og Europa ved inngangen til et nytt århundre*, p. 267.

[8]   B.O. Knutsen, Norge og utviklingen av EUs sikkerhets- og forsvarspolitikk, FFI-Fokus, Oslo: FFI, 2010, p. 5.

[9]   *Ibid.*, p. 9.

materiel and cooperation on defence technology, as when fighter planes from different countries transfer fuel while airborne, and so on. Both officials and cabinet ministers meet in the EDA, and it is the most important meeting place for Norwegian admission to the defence cooperation we wish to take part in, and which our soldiers have to fight alongside.

Great Britain does a U-turn – again

Norway put its faith in Great Britain to protect the Norwegians' interests in exactly the same way as during the dissolution of the union in 1905, the outbreak of the First World War in 1914, the Second World War in 1940, the establishment of Marshall Plan in 1946 and the creation of the Coal and Steel Union in 1950. The British were supposed to be Norway's guarantor against all forms of supranational cooperation on the European continent and safeguard Norway against the EU being given any part in the defence of Europe. But as in 1960, when Great Britain suddenly applied for membership of the EC, the British would again play a trick on Norway. In 1998 Great Britain did the same about-turn because it saw the need to anchor British interests within the new European cooperation. And Norway's approach to European defence policy cooperation had to be re-assessed. As a stop-gap measure the government referred to Norway's associate membership of the Western European Union (WEU) as compensation for a lack of political dialogue with the EU's defence ministers. When the WEU was later integrated into the EU cooperation, however, that was no longer an alternative. This has not been highlighted in the debate on Norwegian defence policy.

Anna Lindh's hug

Vollebæk started to get worried where he was sitting out in the corridor waiting to be allowed in to talk to his colleagues in the EU. Seven hours had now elapsed since the meeting with the EFTA countries was supposed to have started. The time was now getting on for 10 p.m. and the coffee bar, where it was also possible to buy wine or a glass of whisky, was now void of anything reminiscent of food.

The EFTA countries usually came in for a conversation with the EU's foreign ministers *before* the invited cabinet ministers from the candidate countries. That was also the case for those who had signed association agreements with the EU. At that point, however, all the countries of Central and Eastern Europe were queuing up to become members, and the EU presidency wanted to progress discussions that could lead to genuine membership negotiations. The aim was to make one's mark as an effective presidency to one's EU colleagues and leave a legacy in the annals of European history. The agenda was therefore changed at the eleventh hour, and the conversation with the candidate countries' ministers prioritized over the dialogue with the EFTA countries. Thus, Vollebæk remained sitting in the corridor for several hours to come.

The wait was not the only thing making Vollebæk feel uneasy. It was important to catch the discussions and the debate behind closed doors because they included reflections and views from our neighbours. This was of inestimable importance to our own government's attitude towards the EU's new cooperation when it came both to expanding eastwards and to the substance of the new mandate for defence cooperation. Would Norway ask to be allowed to remain part of the EU's defence policy cooperation? Did they want to send Norwegian soldiers to fight alongside the EU countries' forces without Norway being part and parcel of the political discussions prior to such a decision?

During the year, Vollebæk had led the Norwegian presidency of the Organization for Security and Cooperation in Europe (OSCE). There he had enjoyed dealing with the EU's foreign ministers at close quarters. So he had been looking forward to sharing his experiences and impressions of the tense situation in the Balkans.

At 22.10 hours, the door of the meeting hall in the EU's Council of Ministers suddenly flew open. First the Commissioner for External Relations, Chris Patten, came storming out, followed by the recently appointed High Representative of the Union for Foreign Affairs and Security Policy (CFSP), former NATO secretary-general Javier Solana, together with a pack of advisers and security guards. One minister of foreign affairs after another then poured out of the room and swept past Vollebæk and the delegation from the EFTA. Only Swedish Minister of Foreign Affairs Anna Lindh paused to have a chat with her Norwegian colleague.

"What were you talking about that took such a long time?" Vollebæk exclaimed as he gave Anna a warm hug.

"The new defence and foreign-policy cooperation in the EU – it's *tough!*" Lindh replied.

"Yes, I'll need to hear more about it", Vollebæk said.

"You will indeed", Lindh replied, with a twinkle in her eye, "exactly the same way we always get to hear about the NATO meetings".[10]

Vollebæk's smile stiffened as he waved her off. The delegations from Iceland, Liechtenstein and Norway went into the large hall. Of the 15 foreign ministers only a handful remained. It turned out to be a short meeting.

The Storting version

In the *Storting* a year earlier, Vollebæk had proudly related how Norway was contributing to increased stability and security in Europe through OSCE.[11] Norway intended to show Europe what a dependable partner and ally we were, and what values we set store by. The meeting at the EU's Council of Ministers that December evening showed a different version of Norway's role and position. Norway was not admitted to the meeting until the discussions had finished. The EEA Agreement's promise of foreign-policy dialogue – the crux of Norway's political dialogue with the EU – was non-existent in reality.

The EEA Council's meetings were not discussed in the Norwegian Europe Review "*Outside and Inside*"[12] That may be for a number of reasons. One likely reason is that no Norwegian foreign ministers wish to put the poor participation by the EU countries and the Commission in the spotlight. As Jonas Gahr Støre said when confronted with the foreign ministers' scope for manoeuvre in such situations in a debate

---

[10] As assistant to the Deputy Secretary-General of EFTA, I was in the vicinity and witnessed the event.

[11] Norwegian Minister of Foreign Affairs, Knut Vollebæk, Norges formannskap i OSSE, utenriksministerens redegjørelse for *Storting*et, 19 November 1998.

[12] Europautredningen (Norwegian Europe Review), NOU 2012: 2 *Utenfor og innenfor.*

with Iver B. Neumann: "I can't put my cards on the table".[13] And that was precisely the government's quandary in 1994. It could not play the EEA Agreement. Firstly, it would look bad for Norway; and secondly, no one knew how the EEA cooperation would eventually play out and could thus say what a fiendishly parlous agreement we got. The people were hoodwinked.

Yes to what?

Who could know anything of the consequences EU membership would have in 1994? The Norwegian Europe Review "*Outside and Inside*" from 2012 describes people's understanding of what Norway's relationship with the EU means in very brutal terms: "A paradox during the period 1994-2011 is that while all graphs of actual Norwegian association with the EU are rising evenly, the trend in political and general debate, media coverage and knowledge is flat or occasionally falling. *There are not many other areas of Norwegian democracy in modern times where so many have known so little about so much as the politics of Europe.*"

Research into what people knew about the EC cooperation or the EEA Agreement in 1994 is thin on the ground, but knowledge and understanding cannot have been greater than in 2012. The reason is that there was no practical experience to point to for potential implications of the Single Market, or how the EEA Agreement would function. And it must have been even more difficult to understand the difference between EU and EEA membership.

The EU in the year 1994 – a PowerPoint project

In 1994 the EU cooperation's ambitious project for a Single Market – that is, to remove all barriers preventing the free movement of goods, services, capital and people – had barely got off the ground. It was,

---

[13]   S. Ryen, J. Risvik and B. de Carvalho, "Norwegian Ministers of Foreign Affairs Thorvald Stoltenberg, Bjørn Tore Godal, Knut Vollebæk, Thorbjørn Jagland, Jan Petersen and Jonas Gahr Støre in conversation with Jan Egeland", in *Internasjonal Politikk* 1 (1), 2010, pp. 89-114.

and still is, far from complete. People were asked to make up their minds about a project which simply did not exist: Honestly, who could provide a credible answer to what the concrete consequences of opening markets and removing monopolies and government support for traditional sectors and companies would be? No one could say with any certainty whether and to what extent Norwegians would take advantage of the chance to study, work or retire in other EU and EFTA countries or what kind of labour immigration Norway would experience. Many also feared that affluent Germans and Frenchmen would buy up popular seaside haunts along the Norwegian coast. The very notion of "free movement" evoked associations of chaos, invasion and loss of control. The EU's Single Market appeared about as real as a vision of a project or an interesting lecture with a PowerPoint presentation given at a conference. It seemed like an *idée fixe* that keen, well-educated bureaucrats in Brussels had thought up. Predicting the effect that changes to the EU's Single Market might have on our society was a guessing game at best. Lack of knowledge made the EU a much harder cause to sell, a fact which fed through to the day-to-day campaign. The psephologists (electoral scientists) Anders Todal Jenssen and Henry Valen were right when, the year after the referendum, they wrote: "The Yes-voters were less intense in their point of view than the No-side."[14] The simplified message was much simpler to sell than the specialists' insight based on the outcome of month-long, dramatic negotiations. The No-side's simple but effective slogan from 1972 is a good example: "No to selling Norway!". Who among us wished to sell Norway? The reality today is that we sold our right to promote our views and interests in the arenas that determine our economic and political future. Another good example was the drama during the Norwegian Broadcasting Corporation (NRK's) last electoral debate between MPs including Gro Harlem Brundtland and Anne Enger Lahnstein, in which Brundtland lost her temper and accused her opponent of lying.[15] The case was about the potential impact of EU legislation on the protection of employees' rights. The tragic thing was that this debating format extorted a yes/no

---

[14] A.T. Jenssen and H. Valen (ed.), *Brussel midt imot. Folkeavstemningen om EU*, Oslo: Ad Notam Gyldendal, 1995, p. 123.

[15] Europautredningen (Norwegian Europe Review), NOU 2012: 2, debate on NRK (Norwegian Broadcasting Corporation) with Terje Svabø, 25 November 2014.

answer, whereas in reality it was far more complex, of course. We never did get the answer until the Sejersted Committee's Europe Review came out 18 years later in 2012. The report is complex and nuanced, but has a clear conclusion nevertheless: the EU's minimum rules have turned out to provide better protection and stronger rights in a number of areas. The Sejersted Committee even goes as far as to establish that the Norwegian working-life model "in some areas has [...] been developed further so as to offset new dividing lines in the labour market after the EU enlargement in 2004".

The government's slant (for the people and elected representatives)

Norway's ability to influence the EU was discussed in depth in the government's presentation of the EEA Agreement before the *Storting* was due to lend its support to the agreement.[16] The legislative proposal put before the *Storting* explains that participation from Norwegian experts must ensure that the EU-side takes Norwegian points of view into account. In bureaucratic jargon this is described as an "ongoing briefing and consultation process in which the two pillars exchange views on the draft in hand and possible amendments thereto in parallel with consultation and deliberation procedures internal to the EC",[17] and "regulations in the agreement can also be further developed jointly". This means that the EU countries would evaluate Norwegian views *before* negotiating their own compromises and resolutions. They would wait to adopt their own directives, therefore, until they had obtained the views of the EFTA countries. The government's information material stressed that the EEA Agreement would give Norway an opportunity to take part in formulating EU regulations, and in that way soft-pedalled the democratic deficit problem. The Norwegian Ministry of Foreign Affairs' information booklet from September 1994, two months before the referendum, states that "the EEA gives us an opportunity to influence

---

[16] Norwegian parliamentary bill (St.prp.) No. 100 (1991-1992) *Om samtykke til ratifikasjon av Avtale om Det europeiske økonomiske samarbeidsområde (EEA)*, signed in Oporto on 2 May 1992.

[17] *Ibid.*

regulations in those areas covered by the agreement, but not the right to take part in the EU's decision-making process".[18]

It is difficult to know whether to laugh or cry at this description. Today the reality is quite different. The EU countries adopt things, and Norway takes them on without any political influence. When the parliamentary bill was written, the government could not have foreseen that the power ratio between the EU countries and the EFTA countries would become as skewed as 15 to 3, and later 28 to 3. Nevertheless, in 1994 it would seem naive to believe that the twelve EU countries were supposed to *wait* for the six EFTA countries' assessments *before* negotiating their way to final resolutions. The government's portrayal of the EEA was so "politically correct" lest it should have to defend statements that might later undermine the Norwegian people's confidence in the agreement. The description, for example, of Norway's "ability to influence the EU" would turn out to have only shallow roots in reality, where the government talked of a "continuous consultation process" between the EU and the EFTA countries. It would take ten years for any government to concede that the reality was different. A white paper from the Bondevik II government established that "experience from the EEA Committee and its subcommittees suggests that no continuous consultation process will take place before the EU reaches its decisions on the Council and in Parliament, as set down by the EFTA countries before the agreement came into force".[19]

The same can be said of a number of specialist fields. One egregious example is the government's description of the energy field, which in the main was not supposed to be affected by the EEA Agreement. Neither resource management nor licensing policy, to be more explicit. This would prove to be wrong. As pointed out in the 2012 Europe Review, both resource management, the licensing system and market conditions in the petroleum sector were regarded as part of the Single Market and therefore within the ambit of the EEA Agreement.[20] In

---

[18]   "Question and answers on Norway and the EU", Norwegian Ministry of Foreign Affairs, September 1994.

[19]   Norwegian white paper (St.meld.) No. 27 (2001-2002) *Om EØS-samarbeidet 1994-2001*, 22 April 2002, section 4.1.3.6, pp. 88-89.

[20]   Europautredningen (Norwegian Europe Review), NOU 2012: 2, section 19.1.2, pp. 548-550.

the parliamentary bill the government pointed out that "we are at an early stage in the development towards a more coordinated energy policy and more integrated energy markets".[21] That was not sufficient to draw any conclusion that ran counter to the intentions set down by the government.

Another example is related to the economic consequences for the fish processing industry along the coast, an important area that illustrates the difference between being part of the EU's Single Market and being outside of it.

Fish processing has a longstanding tradition in Norway, particularly along the coast to the north. Who could say with any certainty that 120 companies in the white fish industry would have closed down since 1994, while the total processing industry has lost NOK 750 million and 3,200 jobs.[22]

The reason is that the EEA Agreement does not grant favourable tariff treatment for processed fish products of salmon, mackerel, herring, shrimps, prawns, scallops and scampi. On these products, Norwegian fisheries products have punitive duty of anything up to 20 percent imposed, which limits the prospects for exporting Norwegian fish products to Europe in a severely competitive market. A whole Norwegian salmon has 2 percent duty imposed, while a filleted salmon has 13 percent imposed. As a result, nearly all processing of Norwegian salmon takes place elsewhere. Aker Seafoods, Marine Harvest and the Norwegian fish farming trade are therefore investing massively in processing companies within the EU. In 2012 Marine Harvest bought the Polish fish processing company Morpol for more than NOK 900 million.[23] One of the main reasons was that Morpol has a strong presence on the German market, with a market share of 39 percent, whereas Marine Harvest was totally absent. In 2014 Norwegian seafood accounts for 21,000 jobs in the EU. These workplaces would have been

---

[21]   Norwegian white paper (St.prp.) Om saamtykke til ratifikasjon av Avtalen om Det europeiske økonomiske samarbeidsområde, *EØS*, No. 100 (1991-1992).

[22]   Fiskeindustrien i Nord-Norge og Nord-Trøndelag. Bjørn Inge Bendiksen, report 10/2009, March 2009. See http://www.nofima.no/filearchive/Rapport%20 10-2009.pdf, p. 4.

[23]   Marine Harvest, press release from 7 December 2012.

sited in Norway if we had not been subject to the restrictions in the EEA Agreement.

Too good an agreement

The same, if not worse still, applied to the EEA Agreement. There was a very large gap between the government's description and the practical reality. One of the questions raised during the membership debate, both while negotiations were in progress and during the lead-up to the referendum, was whether the EEA Agreement was an adequate and satisfactory substitute for membership of the EU. The late ambassador Eivinn Berg, who was the Norwegian chief negotiator for both the EEA Agreement and the membership negotiations, would later invariably maintain that the EEA Agreement was too good, "so good that people saw no need to take the step into the EU". What he was driving at here in particular, of course, was that the business community's basic need for full participation in the Single Market was chiefly met through the EEA. At the same time, it was an indisputable fact – and one that has been under-communicated both then and at virtually any time since – that the EEA did not grant Norway and the other EFTA countries participation in the decision-making processes as they had been envisioned, not by a long chalk.

Many who were sceptical about membership but nevertheless realized that Norway could not be altogether outside the EU's Single Market for the sake of its own trade and industry, explicitly argued that the Norwegians had got what they needed through the EEA Agreement. The centrist party of the Christian Democrats (KrF) best exemplifies this perhaps. Nor was it a coincidence that Kjell Magne Bondevik (and especially Kåre Gjønnes, a fellow party member and member of the Standing Committee on Foreign Affairs), was among Prime Minister Gro Harlem Brundtland's key supporters when the EEA Agreement was due for approval in the *Storting* with a three-quarters majority. So Brundtland and her government were also faced with a dilemma: At the same time, it had to be argued that the EEA Agreement was sound and right for Norway, and that the agreement was not up to scratch after all. Reading some pivotal documents from this period, like the government's Europe Review from 1992 (just months before the

EEA Agreement was due to be voted on in the *Storting*) and the 1994 white paper on membership from 1994, it is not difficult to see how this enforced balancing act largely guides the description of the EEA Agreement and the relationship between it and EU membership. No one was allowed to "slag off" the EEA Agreement, as they like to put it in the modern vernacular.

It is not altogether unreasonable to claim that there were people who were adherents of the EEA but at the same time opponents of membership, which represents the difference between a No-sayer and a Yes-sayer in the 1994 referendum. Eivinn Berg's evaluation that the EEA Agreement was too good was actually shared by other centrist players too. Jacques Delors had aired the notion of stronger, more structured cooperation between the EC and the EFTA countries in January 1989, presumably to keep Austria, especially, at a distance from the membership it had expressed a desire to have. This was 9 months before the fall of the Berlin Wall, and no one could have predicted what was to happen later that year. Owing to the 1955 agreement with the Soviet Union on the neutrality of Austria, possible Austrian membership was still viewed as a threat to the further development of the foreign and security policy cooperation in the EC. Given the completely new situation that arose during the following months and years, however, this was no longer relevant. Austria, Sweden and Finland applied for membership, as the reader will know. The EEA initiative had thus lost an important part of its very *raison d'être.* What remained was the option of association with the Single Market without membership. Like Eivinn Berg, Delors later expressed the view that the agreement had made it difficult to rally round membership of a country like Norway. And indeed in 2002, in the informal setting of a conversation with Nordic ambassadors in Paris, Delors did state that "the EEA was a strategic mistake".[24]

The EEA Agreement may have been "too good" in the sense that it made it possible to maintain that Norway's economic interests were sufficiently well protected without membership. Delors, however, knew perfectly well – better than anyone, of course – that the agreement certainly was not "up to scratch": the EFTA countries' scope for participating in and influencing the EU's decision-making processes

---

[24]   Reported verbally by a person present at the conversation.

had been reduced to zero during the time the negotiations were in progress. Few talked about this when the EEA Agreement came to be approved by the *Storting*, or when an explanation had to be given as to why it would be right for Norway to go the whole hog and become a member with full rights.

Comparing the 1992 white paper on Norwegian participation in the EEA with the Sejersted Committee's "Outside and Inside", the *Storting* and the Norwegian people can safely be said to have been led right down the garden path.

Heyerdahl won

The only one who knew the true meaning of the difference between EU membership and the EEA Agreement seems to have been Anne Enger's friend, Orkla manager Jens P. Heyerdahl Jnr. According to Statistics Norway's report from June 2013, the price level of groceries and non-alcoholic beverages is 86 percent higher than the EU average.[25] Denmark's price level is 20 percent below that of Norway, while Sweden's is about 22 percent lower.

In summer 2014 a 400 gramme jar of Nora raspberry jam made by Orkla Foods Norway cost Norwegian kroner 29.90. In Sweden it costs Swedish kroner 17.90, while the tariff rate on jam is Swedish kroner 5.35 per kilogramme. A half-litre bottle of mineral water costs Norwegian kroner 18.90 plus a statutory deposit in Norway, whereas in Sweden it costs Swedish kroner 12.90 (approx. Norwegian kroner 11.50), and that despite the price of sugar in Norway being considerably lower than in Sweden and there being no customs duty on mineral water. In Belgium, the same bottle costs euro 1.15 (approx. Norwegian kroner 9). A 74 gramme pack of chocolate swiss roll costs Norwegian kroner 18.90 in Norway. In Sweden, it costs Swedish kroner 13.90 (approx. Norwegian kroner 12.40). 400 grams of finest Belgian milk chocolate costs euro 3.65, or Norwegian kroner 32.

---

[25] SSB, Norge har Europas høyeste matvarepriser, article, 24 June 2013. See http://www.ssb.no/priser-og-prisindekser/artikler-og-publikasjoner/norge-har-europas-hoeyeste-matvarepriser.

A Grandiosa pizza costs Norwegian kroner 110 per kilogramme in Norway. In Sweden, the kilo price for a similar pizza is Swedish kroner 80 (approx. Norwegian kroner 71), while the tariff rate on pizza is just Swedish kroner 5.76 per kilogramme.

In other words, Heyerdahl knew what he was talking about. By properly protecting Norwegian tariff barriers on the most important products, Orkla Foods and Orkla Ingredients have contributed to Orkla becoming a check-out success for big Norwegian investors like Kjell Inge Røkke, Christen Sveaas, Stein Erik Hagen and the National Insurance Fund. Few other Norwegian companies have experienced such turbulent ownership and leadership, which indicates an attractive market with big profits.

In 2006 Orkla was one of six companies that donated a total of NOK 13 million for the construction of the Oslo Centre for Peace and Human Rights, an independent foundation headed by departing Prime Minister Kjell Magne Bondevik. However, in 2011 their support was cut. Bondevik then contacted me in Brussels. He needed help to collect his passport from the Myanmar Embassy, to which he had applied for a visa. In addition, he was keen for advice on how to apply to the EU for money for the centre.

CHAPTER 5

Twelve Expensive Minutes in Brussels That Turned out Profitable

"The EEA is a monster", the former Icelandic Ambassador in Brussels said. The EEA Agreement is so intricate and complicated that no one will ever understand what's going on, how and why. Together with Norway's allies, Iceland and Liechtenstein, tough battles are being fought every single month, more often than not in areas we hear little about.

Borschette-goers

The headed paper really did read "Rome OOc". We glanced up at the board on the wall after we had passed through security control. None of us had heard of the meeting room on the 00th floor. There was just the main entrance, a lift, an escalator and a coffee bar. Guttorm Vik, EFTA's Deputy Secretary-General, had lived away from Norway for long enough to understand that the 0th floor was the same as the Norwegian 1st floor. But 00th floor was new to him too. There was no meeting room in sight. And there was no point either in trying to ask the guard at the information desk behind a crowd of senior officials from Southern Europe due to take part in the Leonardo da Vinci programme's steering committee – one of the fifty other meetings taking place that day. At the meeting, the participants from all the EU countries were supposed to agree on both a draft budget and contents for the Leonardo da Vinci programme, which centred around the exchange of students and teachers at vocational training schools and technical colleges around Europe. The programme was a honeypot for large European educational institutions with a lack of mobility and poor finances. All the parties knew that if they were able to influence the contents of the programme, it would increase their chances of satisfying the requirements in their applications for financial support. The problem was that few of the participants had previously been to the Borschette Centre – that most unappealing of conference centres named after a soldier, an author and the EU Commissioner from Luxembourg: Albert Borschette. These days it is the name of the European Commission's think-tank, where thousands of experts from all over Europe come to listen to, comment on and criticize new proposals for policies and regulations drawn up by Commission officials. Most unlike the EU Council of Ministers' meetings, where finished draft legislation is negotiated and voted on by the member states' governments on the basis of national negotiating positions, meetings at the Borschette Centre are where the very keenest people in every specialist discipline – whether academics, representatives of the business community or NGOs – are invited to help executive officers at the Commission prepare as good a draft as possible. The Commission is at liberty to invite whomever it wishes, from any country whatsoever. It simply has to have the best and the most eminent brains in order to satisfy itself that it has a robust proposal to send to the Council of Ministers and the European Parliament for negotiation and resolution.

In EEA language, this early phase is called the investigative phase. This is where Norwegian experts from the Food Safety Authority, the Maritime Directorate, the Water Resources and Energy Directorate or the Civil Aviation Authority meet their European colleagues and exchange experiences and views on what the Commission's proposals should contain. It is at this stage that Norway can take part in shaping EU regulations; it is here that the government's active Europe policy is played out.

There was a large crowd beneath the new electric board displaying an overview of meetings for that hot summer's day in Brussels: Friday, 29 June 2001. Initials and abbreviations in English and French were not easy to understand for Greeks and Spaniards, who thus pitched up in front of the counter at security control in the hope of finding a compatriot who could explain the way to the right meeting room in their own language. For frequent Borschette-goers, it is a well-known fact that the security guards are Greek, while the meeting room attendants are Italian. For Norwegian experts, this is important to know. By the time they enter the meeting rooms, the attendants will have put up signs for each member state in alphabetical order and in keeping with their own alphabet. That means that Greece (*Ellas*) comes just before Spain (*España*), with Great Britain (*United Kingdom*) and Belgium (*Belgie/ Belgique*) at either end of the room. Generally speaking, the Italian meeting room attendants do not have a particularly detailed knowledge of the EEA Agreement. No one has told them that Norwegian experts also have to be convened to the Commission's expert meetings according to Articles 99, 100 and 101 of the EEA Agreement. The sign marked NORWAY or EFTA will sometimes be found on the windowsill, but as a rule it has to be asked for from the attendants. It is in the third drawer of the receptionist's lefthand set of shelves. Lobby rule number one for Norwegian experts is to remember the Italian phrase: "*Dove è il posto norvegese?*" ("Where's the Norwegian sign?").

With their sign in hand, they enter the meeting room, which is often packed, filled with a jumble of people who have already embarked on informal conversations, coffee in hand. It's a case of knowing what the others think before having to state one's own views during the meeting. Before the EU's great enlargement in 2004, finding a place to sit was easy. Then all the member states sat around the table furthest away, the one shaped like a horseshoe. In the innermost circle sat applicant countries, candidate countries, the EFTA countries and representatives of trade, industry and NGOs. With 28 member states both tables in the horseshoe are completely full as a rule, so the Norwegian expert usually sits on a chair against the wall, behind his or her Swedish colleague, or whomever they happen to know best from previously. This is one of the reasons high-ranking Norwegian senior officials rarely go to meetings in Brussels. Instead they send young, newly trained underlings with degrees from the UK or France who are used to making small talk in English or French.

EEA in practice. Gas, food and fish

Luckily, Guttorm Vik and I got out early. We were not down to attend an expert meeting, but the monthly meeting between the EU and EFTA at which Norway, Liechtenstein and Iceland take over directives which the EU has already negotiated and adopted. In the packed reception area, we quickly realized we would have to find the meeting room ourselves; or rather: it was my job. As the Vice Secretary-General's assistant and note-taker, I was supposed to organize everything, both the practical side of things and the contents, for the meeting, at which the ambassadors and the officials from the EFTA countries were to meet their counterparts on the EU side – especially on a day like this, when we had to defend interests of very great strategic importance to Norway under three different items on the agenda.

Firstly, the EU and Norway had to agree whether the EU gas market directive was going to apply to the Norwegian Shelf and the management of Norway's petroleum resources. The government thought the EEA Agreement was not applicable to the Norwegian Continental Shelf. In addition, the EEA Agreement did not apply to energy or tax policies, both of which were considered areas of national concern. For several years a mounting conflict had been brewing over foreign companies' rights and access to the Norwegian Shelf and to the infrastructure for exporting gas to Europe. From the time oil and gas extraction started, the Norwegian authorities had set up their own negotiating committee reserved purely for Norwegian companies: the Gas Negotiating Committee (GFU). After the Norwegian Ministry of Petroleum and Energy and Norwegian companies had agreed on the division of the production fields, foreign companies were invited in. The European Commission thought this broke the EU's competition laws, and hence did not agree with the Norwegian approach.

Secondly, the EU and Norway had to negotiate Protocol 3 of the EEA Agreement. It is a freestanding protocol that contains the agreement on tariff rates for ready-made and convenience food products. The tariff rates give the Norwegian food industry a chance to protect itself against Swedish and Danish competitors on products like jam, pizza, ice-cream and chocolate. In 2001, the Orkla Group had some 9,000 employees in Norway, while the remaining 2,000 were in the other Nordic countries. Orkla was preoccupied with retaining the high tariff rates because they evened out the price difference in the expensive Norwegian raw materials. The tariff rates were a great annoyance to Swedish and Danish food producers. The food producers had therefore been putting pressure on the Commission's negotiations with Norway.

Thirdly, the EU demanded that it be allowed to send fish from Danish trawlers in transit through Norway. That would entail the Danes, say, being able to send fish from Ålesund to Oslo by trailer without having to sell the fish on the quayside in Ålesund and buying it again at the quayside in Oslo before transporting it to Denmark. Quite unexpectedly, the Commission had raised this issue during the meeting two months earlier, and Norway had been given little time to compose itself. What was at stake here was the monopoly held by *Norges Sildesalgslag* (NSS), a nationwide, self-financed, fishermen-owned sales organization for pelagic fishermen. The organization plays an important role in Norwegian fisheries policy as it determines minimum prices for fish. In practice the *salgslag*, or cooperatives, in Norway act as both an association, an outlet and management.[1]

Of the 86 meetings of the EEA Committee since 1994, this must have been one of the most important of all. The meeting was about managing the family silver: thousands of jobs in the outlying districts and an important principle for Norwegian fisheries policy.

The delegation from EFTA

Having made it safely through security, we went to the coffee bar and ordered a double espresso. The night before we had sat up till half-past one and scrutinized every single word of the items in Norway's Ambassador to the EU's speaking notes. Guttorm Vik's command of words, language and expressions was unique; and with his eye for even the tiniest details we remained seated behind the overcrowded desk in the office, honing the presentations which Einar Bull, the Norwegian Ambassador to the EU, was due to present at the meeting with the EU the following day on behalf of all three EFTA countries. Message and content were based on the outcome of the negotiations between Iceland, Liechtenstein and Norway that same day.

The ambassadors and the heads of officialdom from the EFTA countries had two important tasks. Firstly, they had to ensure that the institutions of the EEA Agreement were working according to plan. Norway could perfectly well arrive at a solution with the Commission at its own bilateral meeting, but the agreement and its institutions would

---

[1] Norwegian government report from 2011, "Råfiskloven – fra kriseløsning til omstridt monopol", by B. Hersoug, P. Christensen and B.-P. Finstad, Norwegian College of Fishery Science (NFH), Universitety of Tromsø.

then be undermined and put out of action. The agreement was still young, and it was important to bolster confidence in the role of the EEA institutions.

Secondly, they were concerned that Norway, Iceland and Liechtenstein's views were coordinated, so that EFTA would then speak as one. Admittedly, the EU Gas Market Directive was not as important for Iceland or Liechtenstein, neither of which has yet struck oil or gas, but it was important that the two small countries not oppose the Norwegian negotiating position.

The preparatory meeting between the three countries was coloured by polite diplomatic turns of phrase, glossing neatly over anything that might resemble conflicts or clashes of interest. And even with just three relatively small EFTA countries, the meetings tended to stretch well into the evening. The time-consuming processes and difficult discussions may partly explain why Norway has always opposed new members of EFTA and the EEA Agreement, be it the Faroes, Slovenia, Andorra or San Marino. With even more countries, even more limited interests, things would simply become unbearable in that little EFTA family.

Rome 00c would prove to be one of the smaller meeting rooms in the Borschette Building. It was situated next to the little coffee bar and was made for in-house meetings for employees of the Commission. It was far smaller than the usual meeting rooms and had no air-conditioning.

First came the prince. The man with the light-blue moustache, Prince Nikolaus of Liechtenstein. He was the ruling Prince of Liechtenstein's younger brother and married to the sister of the Duke of Luxembourg. He was accompanied by Gunter Frommelt, who was number two of just three diplomats in the principality's delegation to the EU. Prince Nikolaus wore an almost permanent smile, particularly in markedly demanding and unpleasant situations. And people could not help but smile in his presence, also because there was something genuinely elegant and regal about him. He was irreproachable, unassailable and every inch the aristocrat. Even when the European Commission threatened to exclude Liechtenstein's college of architecture from the list of mutually approved educational establishments because far too many Germans took the three-year architects' programme there instead of the five-year one back home, the prince just sat with a broad smile, without saying much, right until he got what he wanted.

Just behind him came the Icelandic ambassador, Gunnar Snorri Gunnarsson. Like many Icelandic diplomats, Gunnarsson was particularly cultured, well-read and, of course, spoke good French. At functions back at home he would often sit at the piano strumming a few notes. Gunnarsson did not once take the floor without starting off with a historical anecdote, preferably from the Icelandic sagas, generally with great success – something that earned him great sympathy before he delivered a string of bad news. It was an elegant way of deflecting attention away from the substance of his address or a diplomatic attempt to camouflage the message because his brief from Reykjavik as to what Iceland would make of things was not yet clear. As a rule, Iceland was far behind in most areas of the EEA cooperation, whether it was political preparation of directives, translation of legislative texts or quite simply the lack of a mandate from Reykjavik on the stance to be taken by Iceland on current issues. With him the Icelander had two colleagues from the Icelandic delegation in Brussels and one diplomat from Reykjavik.

A couple of minutes later the Norwegian delegation arrived with Ambassador Einar Bull at the helm, followed by a dozen colleagues, or rather specialist advisers from the Norwegian EU delegation, the Ministry of Foreign Affairs and often other Oslo-based ministries or directorates involved. With the agenda full of matters of special interest to Norway, it was only natural that the ministries sent their own representatives to get information about the EU's views and reactions first-hand. The delegation from Norway, in other words, was six times the size of Liechtenstein's and four times the size of Iceland's, which was quite normal considering the countries' size. Einar Bull was particularly well liked, both on the EU side and among EFTA colleagues. He was always cheerful and pleasant, and he took time out to greet everyone. Ambassador Bull used to say that his job was like running a village shop in the old days: "I deal in a bit of fish, a bit of steel, some foodstuffs, and then a bit of finance." In a nutshell, all the problem areas between Norway and the EU. The man from Alta's disarming demeanour has saved Norwegian industry and the kingdom a great deal of money and conflicts. Einar Bull was also a dyed-in-the-wool European. His first job after graduating from the Norwegian School of Economics in

Bergen was as secretary-general to the European Movement under the leadership of Halvard Lange.

There was not much of a buzz about the meeting room so early in the morning. Everyone sat waiting for the EU delegation. It consisted of three people, headed by the Swede who was later to become the EU ambassador in Oslo, Percy Westerlund, together with the taciturn but razor-sharp Finn Jussi Närvi and their small department's German secretary Evelyn. There were three of them, and twenty-three of us.

The EEA Committee

The tone was generally jovial and friendly at meetings of the EEA Committee, especially between Westerlund and Bull, who had known each other well for many years in Brussels. They had also negotiated the EEA Agreement, alongside Austrians, Swiss and Finns, and EU membership immediately after that. It would be different nowadays.

Conditions were particularly cramped on one side of the table in the small meeting room, and the delegation from the EFTA countries had to sit behind one another, with only the ambassadors and EFTA's secretary-general in the first row. On the other side the three EU representatives sat in the centre, surrounded by 15 empty chairs. Space had been left in case diplomats from the EU's member states came to the meeting. The aim of the EEA Committee meeting was to smooth the way for dialogue between the countries of the EU and EFTA: together they were supposed to discuss considerations and deliberations regarding the content of the directives the EU countries were in the process of adopting at their own meetings. It was here that the EFTA countries were to put forward points of view, be heard and talk over matters relating to the Single Market of which they were part. As at all meetings held at the Brochette Centre, the name badges for each EU country were strung across the table. In this instance, however, there were no diplomats sitting behind the badges. The chairs were empty. No one turned up. The reason was that none of the EU countries assigned priority to taking part in EEA Committee meetings because they were about matters they had already finished negotiating and had adopted. Instead the diplomats with the EU countries' permanent representations (as their embassies are called in EU-ese) were preoccupied among themselves with negotiations about new directives. Since the EEA Committee's remit involved directives they had *already* adopted but had to formally hand over to the EFTA countries, they entrusted the task to the Commission's representatives because, under the agreement, the Commission nonetheless has to take the floor on behalf of all the EU countries. The member states' diplomats had discussed the EEA Committee's agenda with Percy Westerlund and Jussi Närvi beforehand.

In practice that means that the diplomats with the Norwegian EU delegation are precluded from meeting their colleagues in the EU countries while all seated together at the same meeting. This is because the Norwegian diplomats do not have access to the EU countries' internal meetings. They just meet when they request a meeting of their own or in social settings.

"Can we adopt the agenda?" Westerlund asked, and the meeting was off. The first minutes were spent on routine things like approving the minutes from last time and the reports from the advisory committee that had been discussing and approving how EU rules were to be embodied in the EEA Agreement. Then came the list of EU directives that would require their own parliamentary hearing in Norway, Iceland or Liechtenstein. When an EU directive requires a change in law, the government has to table a white paper with subsequent consultation deadlines, committee and plenary debate, and resolution. The EFTA countries then have six months' extra time to introduce the new rules into national law. Since the EEA Agreement entered into force in 1994, the *Storting* has had to amend Norwegian law just short of 300 times to adapt it to EU directives. The other 10,000 EU rules have all been incorporated through regulations, i.e. without any parliamentary debate.

Ambassador Bull looked across to his colleagues from Iceland and Liechtenstein, who both gave a consenting nod:

"Yes, we can", Bull replied, allowing Westerlund to carry on reading out the pre-typed speaking notes.

"We can adopt the incorporation of ten EEA Committee decisions in the agreement, which contains eleven pieces of legislation." Each EEA Committee decision contained a regulation, a directive, an EU programme or an agreement to participate in a new EU agency. This way,

Norway, Iceland and Liechtenstein avoid ceding any legal sovereignty, as they would have been allowed to do if EU members. On the EEA Committee they make their own decision about including the directive in the agreement and then in their own national legislation. This happens despite the contents of the directive having been negotiated without the involvement of the EFTA countries and the EEA Agreement stipulating that all directives must be included in the agreement.

Ending Norwegian gas preferences

It was not till the fifth item on the agenda, "Handling of outstanding pieces of legislation," that a certain apprehension could be sensed on the EFTA countries' side of the table. It concerned the directives the EU had adopted, but without achieving a consensus as to how to work them into the EEA Agreement. In the Norwegian camp, there was great tension as to what Westerlund would say about the directive topping the list: the gas market directive. The directive would place Norwegian companies on an equal footing with other companies from EU countries in terms of gas distribution. Norway had given up any hope of being able to refuse to include it in the agreement, i.e. veto it. Instead they had asked to have a transitional period of six years. When the answer was no, Norway asked for three years, which the EU countries did not accept either. Would the EU be able to accept one year?

Westerlund was always cheerful and friendly, even if rather quietly spoken and laid-back. Every time Ambassador Bull presented a request for a Norwegian special requirement, the Swede replied that he would have to talk it over with his colleagues in the EU countries. In practice that meant that Westerlund would bring up the Norwegian requirement at a separate meeting of the EU's Council of Ministers with only the EU's member states in attendance. For while the EU and the EFTA countries met every last Friday of the month, Westerlund held a meeting with representatives from all the EU countries every other Wednesday of the month in order to give the Commission a negotiating mandate for discussions with the EFTA countries. This is precisely where an important dimension of the EEA Agreement's democratic deficit is not particularly well known. Not even in the Sejersted Committee's final report *Utenfor og innenfor*[2] on Norway's relationship with the EU was this issue mentioned. Most people know that Norway has no opportunity to take part in negotiations where the EU countries adopt laws and regulations which Norway has undertaken to introduce without knowing what they contain. Once the EU regulation has been adopted and forwarded to the EFTA countries for review and incorporation in the EEA, the agreement stipulates that Norway and the other two countries can request minor changes to the regulation in order to adapt parts of the directive to conditions in their home country. In some cases, it is also a matter of securing a few essential derogations (dispensations) or transitional arrangements, as in the case of the gas market directive.

It is far less well known that representatives of the Norwegian authorities have no way of explaining Norway's situation to the EU countries and making sure they understand the rationale behind Norway's requests for derogations from EU regulations, as the EU countries themselves do. Instead the Commission puts the arguments to the EU's own member states on our behalf. This is a major paradox: the Commission is responsible for introducing the EU rules adopted, in the correct manner and at the correct time, in all the EU countries. Even if the Commission were to do its best, out of sympathy for Norway, to negotiate on Norway's behalf, it is obviously most concerned with ensuring that the acquis adopted by its own negotiations over a number of years in the Council of Ministers and the European Parliament is implemented in the EFTA countries as well. It is as if EFTA's Surveillance Authority, ESA, which is responsible for ensuring that the EU's body of laws is properly implemented in Norwegian law, were to be responsible for arguing that a directive should *not* be followed.

Ambassador Bull took the floor first, giving an account of the Norwegian government's view of the application of the EEA Agreement. Norway had previously signalled that its chief wish was to keep the directive out of the agreement or to be exempted from parts of the directive, enabling it to carry on its present practice as regards managing its gas resources. At one time, Norwegian authorities used to sit down just with Norwegian companies to coordinate the marketing and sale of Norwegian gas. No foreign companies were allowed to take part.

---

[2]   Europautredningen (Norwegian Europe Review), NOU 2012: 2.

Norway had therefore felt compelled to disband the gas negotiating committee, under which the Norwegian authorities had treated Norwegian and foreign companies differently. Companies in the EU and Norway enjoyed equal status, and in this way, Ambassador Bull claimed, Norway had satisfied the directive's chief requirement concerning equal treatment of the petroleum companies in Norway and the EU. Westerlund leant slightly further forward than usual and told ambassadors Gunnarsson, Prince Nikolaus and Bull that he had had discussions with the EU countries the previous Wednesday in the EU Council of Ministers' working party responsible for the EU's relationship with the EFTA countries.

"I must disappoint you and inform you that little appreciation was expressed for the Norwegian request," Westerlund said. "Several of the EU's member states, like the Netherlands, Great Britain and Denmark, were in the same situation as Norway. After much pressure from the Commission and the other countries they had agreed to open up the petroleum services market by dismantling national negotiating fora, which were in violation of the directive. They therefore saw no reason why Norway should be granted a derogation which they themselves had not been given."

Ambassador Bull cast a quick look back to the representative of the Ministry of Petroleum and Energy, who nodded resignedly. This was the end of the road. For more than three years after the EU had adopted the directive, the ministry had attempted to do its utmost to keep the directive out of the EEA Agreement, but in vain.

The EU's goal was to open up the European gas market to increased competition by counteracting the concentration of companies and monopolistic trends in the market. One implication of this was that gas buyers would be free to choose which gas supplier they wished to buy from, and the gas transportation pipeline system would be accessible to anyone wishing to use it. As described by the Norwegian Europe Review, the problem for Norway was, firstly, that it had no appetite for free competition and third-party access to the gas pipelines on the Norwegian Shelf. Secondly, the directive indirectly affected the long-term contracts which Norwegian suppliers had with European buyers. Since production on the Norwegian Shelf entailed large-scale investment, the emphasis was on securing a sizable volume of export contracts.[3] The new EU rules would force Norwegian authorities to treat all companies equally, which might mean lower revenues for Norwegian companies and increased uncertainty surrounding price trends.

"We understand. We are aware of the negotiations between the Commission and the Norwegian authorities on this matter. We have made it clear to the Commission that the directive will be implemented without any further delays. Our gas market will be altered in accordance with the directive," Ambassador Bull replied. That was the diplomat in Einar Bull coming out, for although his allegiance lay with his employer, the government of Norway, he was absolutely clear that the battle was lost and that it was now a matter of showing that we respected the ground rules and the intent of the agreement.

"Thank you", Westerlund said in his concise manner.

The EU gas market directive was considered a large and important loss in Norway's relationship with the EU. More latterly, most players – companies, economists and authorities alike – have concluded that treating all European players on the Norwegian Shelf equally was instrumental in boosting efficiency on the Shelf. The result was higher revenues for both the state and the companies. Most recently in June 2014, ten top Norwegian industrial players, including NHO, Norwegian Industry, the Shipowners' Association and the Association of Local and Regional Authorities (KS), sent a letter in which they asked the government to introduce competition into the market for pipelines and liquefied natural gas (LNG), where Norway had been granted a ten-year transitional scheme. The reasoning is that they think the players on the Norwegian gas market need and benefit from competition in the market. It will make for efficient use of society's resources. Attitudes towards the industry, the authorities and the political environment would again change considerably with the concrete experience gained from introducing the EU gas market directive. Once again, Europe was contributing to Norwegian prosperity.

---

[3]   Europautredningen (Norwegian Europe Review), NOU 2012: 2, section 19.1.1, pp. 546-548.

Jam, chocolate and pizza

"The next item of business is 'Protocol 3: negotiations on trade in processed agricultural products.'"

Westerlund referred yet again to the conversation he had had with the EU's member states the week before, though everyone on the EFTA side knew it was only about Sweden. He made reference to Protocol 3 of the EEA Agreement, in which the parties had agreed to gradually equalize differences in raw material prices. It is called the "raw material price compensation system", abbreviated in Norwegian to RÅK. These are raw materials used in processed agricultural products (PAP), which is to say baked goods and sugar goods such as jam, margarine, chocolate, pizza and ice-cream.

The case had been dragging on for years, and the EU side had been showing signs of losing patience. The mood among the Norwegian delegation was resigned and somewhat frustrated.

After the Commission and Norway had been negotiating for several years and finally reached agreement on the new tariff rates, the Swedes suddenly protested. They felt the Commission had been too indulgent over Norwegian demands. The tariff rates on goods like jam, chocolate and pizza were still far too high for Swedish products to be able to muscle in on the Norwegian market. The tariff rates acted as trade barriers to the export of Swedish groceries to Norway. Following powerful pressure from the Swedish authorities, the Commission had to ask for the negotiations to be re-opened.

The Ministry of Foreign Affairs in Oslo had contacted its Swedish colleagues in Stockholm, asking them to appreciate that the Norwegian tariff rates had to be maintained. Jobs were at stake in the outlying districts. They received no clear answer from Stockholm, however. As the Swedish ambassador to the EU at the time, Gunnar Lund, said at a meeting with the Social Democrats in the European Parliament: "In Stockholm good neighbourliness is paramount, while in Brussels anything goes."

For this reason, the Swedes had taken the floor at the preparatory meeting between the Commission and the EU countries, requesting that negotiations be resumed. The fact that Westerlund himself was Swedish was no disadvantage to the Swedish negotiators. No other member states took the floor during the meeting. They found it quite natural for Sweden to ask the Commission for help in promoting their interests *vis-à-vis* a country *outside of the EU.*

After several meetings and intense pressure from the EU side, Norway had to concede to a review clause, stipulating an additional 3 percent reduction in duty within five years. Now Westerlund wanted to know whether the result was acceptable.

"We can accept that," Ambassador Bull had to say, on instructions from Norway.

Only eight minutes had elapsed, and it was starting to get extremely hot in the meeting room, which also lacked oxygen. It did not bode well; the worst was yet to come.

Fish in transit

At the EEA Joint Committee's March meeting, completely out of the blue, the Commission had raised a complaint it had received from the Danish authorities about the transit of fish through Norway. The Danes thought Norway had no right to demand that Danish trawlers fishing in international waters outside of Norway should not be permitted to land the fish in a Norwegian port in order to transport it in transit overland to Oslo before it was sent home to Denmark. On the quays of Norwegian ports, *Sildesalgslaget* had demanded that it be allowed to buy portions of the catch at less than market price in order to grant permission for the fish to be transported through Norway. Denmark and the Commission considered this behaviour to be at odds with Protocol 9 of the EEA Agreement on trading in fish.

The Norwegian delegation was up in arms over the move by the EU. They considered the matter to have been concluded during the 1992 negotiations with the EU when there was no consensus to include trading in fish in the EEA Agreement. If the EU did not admit fish without customs duty, the EU could not expect to gain access to Norwegian markets without observing the rules of the Norwegian market. Norway therefore felt it was unfair to revisit this issue now. Meanwhile, the Danes' anger at being forced to sell cheaply to Norway's *Sildesalgslag* had not abated – on the contrary. Their frustration had grown, and now

Danish diplomats had asked the Commission to straighten things out on the EEA Committee.

The tactic worked. Whatever angle Norway chose to consider the matter from, there was no getting away from the fact that the combination of *Sildesalgslaget's* monopoly and the demand to be allowed to buy the fish at below market price was not very smart.

The Commission demanded an explanation as to what regulations gave Norway's *Sildesalgslag* the authority to exact such payment. For the first time a degree of commitment was heard in Westerlund's tone of voice, when he virtually insinuated that the *Sildesalgslaget's* conduct was reminiscent of mafia conditions. What Ambassador Bull himself thought of the matter will remain unsaid.

Bull tackled the situation neatly by thanking Westerlund for the request before giving the floor to Oda Helen Sletnes, his second-in-command at the EU delegation, who later became President of ESA and then ambassador again. She related that Norway was in the process of writing a memo explaining the situation, which would be delivered to the Commission on Subcommittee number 1 – a subdivision of the EEA Committee. Bull just needed to glance at Westerlund's reaction when he heard Sletnes say how Norway was trying to play for time. He knew the game was over. Then he pressed the red button on the microphone:

"We'll take care of it," he said. "*You have my word.*"

Norway would later manage to peg the reform of Norway's *Sildesalgslag* to the EEA membership fee. This was a hazardous amalgamation of trade policy because it sets a precedent for horse-trading between fisheries interests and Norway's contribution to social and economic levelling in Europe.

"Thank you," Westerlund said again. "The meeting is adjourned. See you next month."

I looked at the clock. The entire session had taken twelve minutes. We packed our cases and dried the sweat from our foreheads. Then we walked through security control, left the Borschette Building and went our separate ways. In that short time, Norway had renounced sovereignty of the gas market, agreed to lower tariff rates on food products and pledged unpaid access for fish in transit. Today there is nothing to suggest that Norway suffered any harm from yielding to the

EU's demands. The demands were even sensible and advantageous for both Norwegian industry and the consumer. Statoil and Orkla have been subject to increasing competition, which they have coped with and grown from. Norway's *Sildesalgslag* has since abolished the transit of fish pending a new agreement on EEA membership fees. Politically, it must have been the most costly twelve minutes Norway has ever experienced.

Norway, the EU, gas and the future

There are few places where Norwegian non-participation in the EU's decision-making body, or rather the possibility of having one-on-one discussions with colleagues from the member states, has had greater consequences for Norway than the petroleum sector. The reason is that this is where clashes of interest are most obvious. One of our most respected experts in this field, Professor Dag Harald Claes from the University of Oslo, has written that the gas market emerged early on as a central target for the Commission's desire for increased liberalization and competition on the energy market. It was a market characterized by large companies that dominated negotiations and controlled the transport of gas through the high-pressure network in Europe. Moreover, many of the companies were publicly owned.[4]

While the EU countries were wrapping up negotiations on the contents of the gas market directive, the government was waging a number of offensives to try to gain a hearing for Norwegian views. Utilizing the government's active Europe policy, all formal and informal channels were used to promote Norwegian views. In the discussion at the *Storting* the Labour Party's Minister of Foreign Affairs, Bjørn Tore Godal, reported the reactions Norwegian diplomats and he himself got:

"Every time I talk to ministers in the EU about this [gas market directive], they look at me as if I come from another planet. They don't get what I'm on about".[5]

There is little to suggest that this clash of interests has changed over time.

---

[4]   EEA-avtalen og norsk energipolitikk, Ole Gunnar Austvik and Dag Harald Claes, Europautredningen (Norwegian Europe Review), subreport No. 8.

[5]   Minutes of *Storting*'s EEA Committee, 22 April 1997.

Minister Godal's experiences were echoed in a statement by former Statoil CEO Helge Lund in the Norwegian business paper *Dagens Næringsliv* in November 2013: "Talking to politicians from the EU countries is like talking to a brick wall."[6] That comment was made in an interview about the EU's understanding of the role that natural gas from the Norwegian Shelf can play for the EU's greenhouse gas emissions. The government and Statoil claim that if the EU substitutes Norwegian gas for energy production from coal, CO_2 emissions will drop drastically. The proposal is not without its problems, however. Firstly, there is no EU country that wishes to increase its dependence on natural gas imports. The reason is simple: the price of natural gas is roughly double that of coal.

The gas market directive was especially difficult for Norway to take on because it would change the way sales of gas from the Shelf were organized. The directive instructed the government to dismantle a committee where Norwegian companies could negotiate solely with Norwegian authorities on both extraction and sales contracts. The EU's objective was to liberalize the European gas market by laying down common ground rules that would give all companies from all EU and EFTA countries equal rights on the market.

An important feature of the EEA Agreement is that it gives representatives of the Norwegian authorities an opportunity to take part in the Commission's preparatory, or decision-shaping, phase. This is the very first phase in drawing up EU regulations: the Commission's draft that will subsequently be negotiated and adopted by the EU's Council of Ministers, where the governments of the member states sit, and in the European Parliament. This preparatory phase is when, as all Norwegian governments since 1994 have stressed, our civil service must improve its performance. The preparatory phase involves the Commission inviting experts from the EU countries' authorities, EFTA countries like us, and sometimes even the business community and civil society. This is the chance for Norwegian government experts to discuss EU rules together with colleagues from EU member states. When the Commission has listened to the advice and, more often than not, the criticism of the experts, it finishes off the draft proposal and submits it to the decision-making bodies.

---

[6] From article in *Dagens Næringsliv*, quoted on Hegnar.no on 30 November 2013.

The Norwegian Ministry of Petroleum and Energy's delegates worked hard to gain sympathy for Norwegian points of view in formulating the draft gas market directive. However, the situation came to a head early on in the phase. Torvild Aakvaag, former director-general of Norsk Hydro, was constantly stating that the EU's policy in this field *vis-à-vis* Norway was an "attack on Norwegian sovereignty",[7] which said a lot about the intensity of the clashing interests.

The gas market directive negotiations coincided with accusations that Statoil and Hydro had been operating illegal price-fixing, and the Commission was threatening to hand out large fines. So Norway was cornered and had little choice but to accept the EU's demands.

The EU regulation most feared by the government and the oil companies was the Petroleum Exploration Directive, under which Norway had to treat Norwegian and the EU countries' companies equally in its distribution of oil and gas extraction licences. The hearing in the EU coincided with a revision of the regulation at home in Norway. In that sense, we were in step with the EU. It also coincided with the period when Norway had completed its membership negotiations up to the referendum on 28 November 1994. During this period the Norwegian Ministry of Petroleum and Energy, like all other ministries, invited people to sit in on and take part in the Council of Ministers' hearing of the Commission's proposal, exactly as if Norway was a member of the EU. In the Norwegian Europe Review the Sejersted Committee says this gave the authorities "considerable influence over the formulation of the directive," and "[f]or the Norwegian authorities, who were highly sceptical of the directive during its early phase, the final directive therefore became far simpler to relate to."[8]

During negotiations on the gas market directive several years later, the government did not have this option. That goes to show how important participation is.

In the case of the gas market directive, Norway suffered its greatest political defeat to date in our relationship with the EU. After the event, it must be said that few people today regret this result. The subreport to the Norwegian Europe Review establishes that opening up the gas

---

[7]   *Aftenposten*, 1 October 2001.
[8]   Europautredningen (Norwegian Europe Review), NOU 2012: 2, p. 553.

market to competition and third-party access to the gas distribution infrastructure have contributed to making the Norwegian petroleum sector competitive and more resilient.

Whatever the consequences of introducing the gas market directive, it did provide a brutal demonstration of power in the relationship between the parties to the EEA Agreement and show that Norway is powerless when it stands alone against an EU that has already spent several years negotiating its way to a common approach. As Professor Øyvind Østerud, head of the Power and Democracy report from 2003, said: "The gas dispute with the EU illustrated that, as a producer, Norway had lost power."[9]

At a petroleum conference in 2002 Dag Harald Claes stated that "in the years ahead we shall also see the EU attempting to use whatever power it may have over Norwegian energy policy to promote its consumer interests, and furthermore to divert as much as possible of the income streams into the consumer countries' coffers".[10] He could not be more right. The EU's imminent energy union will assume great consequences for Norwegian petroleum activities.

---

[9]   Makt- og demokratiutredningen. The Norwegian Oil Industry Association (OLF) and the Research Council of Norway jointly organized the conference "Olje og makt" ["Oil and Power"] in Oslo on 12 September 2002.

[10]   *Ibid.*

PART 3

NORWAY IN THE EUROPE OF THE FUTURE

CHAPTER 6

EU Climate Funds

For most people, the EU seems to be something remote, utterly untouchable and bureaucratic. In practice, the EU cooperation is no worse than any other national decision-making system, with ministries and legislative bodies surrounded by a series of special-interest organizations. It is perfectly possible to influence its outcomes, but you must have a good network and know how to work the system. In partnership with a broad-based alliance, Bellona succeeded in setting up the EU's most important funding of climate technology. That was ascertained by the Council of Europe at the meeting on 23 October 2014. This is the story of how it came about.

March can be one of the loveliest months in Brussels. It is usually the time for the first outdoor lunches at the restaurants along the newly remodelled Place du Luxembourg in front of the European Parliament at the heart of the EU district. Lunch outdoors was also the plan on Wednesday, 16 March 2003, after Bellona had held its first public hearing at the European Parliament on the climate-friendly technology "CO_2 capture and storage" (CCS). Lunch outdoors did not materialize. Two events put a stop to that. Firstly, snow had fallen during the night and lay like a thin, paralyzing carpet over the whole city. In Brussels snowfall is synonymous with traffic chaos, a shortage of taxis and long delays on all public communications. Secondly, the news came that American troops had started the invasion of Iraq without a mandate from the United Nations Security Council (UNSC). Naturally enough, that led to vehement reactions from the members of the European Parliament. Six weeks previously, the Parliament had adopted a harshly worded resolution condemning the USA's plans to topple Saddam Hussein's regime. Twelve introductory speakers from the USA, Great Britain and Norway who should have been attending Bellona's CCS hearing were now weather-bound outside the Floris Arlequin Hotel on the *Grand Place* waiting in vain for their taxis and failing to get to the parliament building on time. Several invited EMPs, assistants and advisers also failed to turn up because they had been convened to an extraordinary plenary meeting to discuss the invasion of Iraq. It was no ordinary day on the job, but it would prove nevertheless to be a milestone in Bellona's EU work.

That morning it was seething with people in the entrance lobby to the European Parliament, which was more reminiscent of a Cairo souk, with a jumble of politicians from all over Europe, senior officials, journalists and lobbyists. Security control did not have the wherewithal to handle the turn-out. At that time all portables and laptops had to be registered too, which was particularly time-consuming. The chaos was complete. With a delay of approximately three-quarters of an hour, MEP Claude Turmes came dashing into the meeting room to The Greens' party group in the European Parliament to welcome attendees and open the hearing.

In autumn 2002, prior to the CCS hearing in the European Parliament, Bellona manager Frederic Hauge and I reached out to one of the advisers closest to EU Commissioner for Environment Margot Wallström. The aim was to engage the Commission in the work of promoting carbon capture and storage in the EU member states. There was a need for both our own regulations on CO_2 storage and resources for researching into and building demonstration plants. During the meeting Hauge emphasized the world's harmful dependence on fossil fuels, explained how CCS technology works and what role technology can play alongside the other measures in the EU's work to cut greenhouse gas emissions. Wallström's adviser did not particularly agree with the technology. He replied by saying that, first and foremost, the Commission wished to introduce a technology-neutral trading system with emission quotas. If polluters have to pay for every tonne of CO_2 they emit, they will have a strong financial incentive to reduce their emissions, whatever technology they use. The total number of emission quotas can be reined in with time, thereby reducing the total level of emissions. In addition, the Commission wished to promote incentives and technologies for increased energy streamlining and the production of renewable energy sources. The adviser's understanding of the need for CCS was surprisingly scanty, if not non-existent. On the way home from the meeting we realized that we had to come up with a new strategy. It would have been easier if we had been able to talk to a commissioner from Norway, who would have been on side with CCS in light of the great debate in 2000, when the Bondevik government had to resign because a majority in the *Storting* wanted to build gas-fired power stations without CCS technology. In no other country had CCS figured so highly on the political agenda as in Norway. The EU had no commissioners at that time with any knowledge or interest in highlighting the need for CCS at a political level. Nor were there any Norwegian EMPs who could introduce CCS at the Parliament's environmental or energy committee; and at any rate no Norwegian cabinet ministers or representatives of the authorities on the EU's Council of Ministers, to which Norway had no access. We had to do the job ourselves, but how and by approaching whom?

From the time Bellona Europe was set up in 1996, right after the Norwegian referendum on EU membership, Frederic Hauge and his colleagues Thomas Nilsen, Igor Kudrik and Nils Bøhmer had actively worked at close quarters with the EU institutions and organized hearings at the European Parliament to present and discuss Bellona's work on scrapping the Russian nuclear fleet and managing the nuclear waste on the Kola Peninsula. The Nikitin Affair, in which the KGB jailed the former Russian submarine captain and author of Bellona reports, had also attracted a great deal of attention and mobilized widespread support among many key MEPs in Central Europe. Nikitin was nominated for the Sakharov Prize, the Parliament's well-known human rights award, several times.

Since 1996 the European Parliament had acquired considerably greater power and influence in the EU through both the Amsterdam and the Nice treaties, giving Parliament joint determination in new areas. This development, together with Bellona's broad-based interface and network in Parliament, led to an important strategic decision: we decided to use the European Parliament as an arena for raising awareness and appreciation, and for promoting Bellona's political message.

The day after the meeting with Commissioner of Environment Wallström's adviser, I contacted the office of Claude Turmes, the trendsetting green politician. He was an MEP that Bellona had invited to inspect conditions at the atomic waste depots in Murmansk. We agreed to meet and discuss the possibility of presenting CCS in the Parliament.

A long-haired former Greenpeace activist, Turmes was in his first term as a member of the European Parliament for the party group that gathered together all the environmental parties in the EU countries, The Greens. Basically, Turmes was not especially enthusiastic about CCS, though he did admit to knowing little about it. But he was interested in taking a closer look at innovative solutions that could promote the introduction of the hydrogen society. By swapping conventional combustion engines powered by polluting petrol in cars, boats, planes and other motorized machines for fuel cell engines powered by hydrogen, up to 30-40 percent of the world's CO_2 emissions could be eliminated. That is necessary if the world is to reach the UN's target of an 80-90 percent reduction in relation to 1990 emission levels. It will take a reduction of that order to keep the globe's temperature rise below 2°C. There are a number of challenges to developing the hydrogen economy. One is the difficulty of storing hydrogen. Another is the lack of production volume. Hydrogen is an energy carrier, just like electricity. That is to say that hydrogen takes energy from where it is generated to where it is consumed; or "from well to wheel", as they also say. A society powered by hydrogen will require vast amounts of energy, and Turmes feared that energy produced by wind, sun and other renewable sources would take too long. It would postpone the technological development needed to get the hydrogen society off the ground. Europe's car industry, headed up by familiar marques like BMW, Opel, Mercedes and Renault, has always stated that it is ready to produce cars with fuel cell engines powered by hydrogen, but the lack of filling stations with a supply of hydrogen makes it impossible to get large-scale car production started. Petroleum companies like Shell, Total and Statoil fall back on exactly the same explanation, only in reverse: they are keen to build hydrogen filling stations along the roads but point out that there are no cars to put the hydrogen into. In order to try and break this "chicken and egg" situation, Turmes was interested in the possibility of removing CO_2 from fossil energy sources, i.e. generating energy from coal and gas without emitting CO_2, and then speeding up hydrogen production. This is the context in which CCS carbon capture and storage entered the picture. One of the capture technologies for CCS can produce huge quantities of hydrogen from oil, coal and gas. Turmes wanted to learn more about this, and so we agreed on the title of the hearing: "The Road to the Hydrogen Society".

During the two and a half hour long hearing Bellona showcased the need for the EU to start orchestrating the development of CCS. If the world is to succeed in stabilizing temperature changes at 2°C by the end of the century, the UN's climate panel says that greenhouse gas emissions must be cut by 80-95 percent by 2050. If the EU is going to shoulder its share of the emission reductions, increasing the production of renewable energy and introducing energy efficiency measures will not be enough. European industry will still rely on being able to use fossil fuels like coal and gas, and in order to prevent industry moving to countries without climate measures, Europe will have to develop technology that can make those countries competitive in a carbon-restricted world. In a carbon-restricted world, where it will be expensive to emit CO_2, CCS technology can make an important contribution to helping industry remain competitive as compared with other regions and remain in Europe.

The EU also needs to think of European energy and the equipment industry's competitiveness vis-à-vis the USA, China and the rapidly growing economies of Southeast Asia and South America. Unless Europe initiates the development of CCS technology, Chinese industry, for example, will be able to develop CCS technology first, thus gaining a head-start and outcompeting European industry when CCS may eventually but quickly become a prerequisite for the European power and industry sector. At the hearing, several American and European companies presented their concrete experience of capturing and transporting CO_2. Statoil's presentation of its experience of storing CO_2 at the Sleipner Field in the North Sea was one of the most pivotal contributions at the hearing. Until then Statoil was the only company in the world that had any hands-on experience of storing CO_2. They had been storing one million tonnes of CO_2 every year since 1996, two kilometres under the seabed. The natural gas Statoil was recovering on Sleipner contained too much CO_2, which had to be separated off before the gas could be transported to market in Europe. When the Norwegian authorities introduced a CO_2 tax on the Shelf, Statoil figured it was cheaper to send the CO_2 back down to where it had been brought up. Due to strict security measures at Statoil in connection with the USA's imminent invasion of Iraq, Statoil's representative had to send his regrets. The solution was that a Bellona employee read out Statoil's paper and presented the PowerPoint presentation Statoil had made, which illustrated the company's experience with CO_2 storage.

The discussion after the presentations would prove to be the most important part of the hearing. The Greenpeace representative sat surprisingly still. By contrast, the representatives we had invited from the Commission's Directorate-General for Research and Development did not, and likewise those from the Directorate-General for Energy, Environment and Trade. In dribs and drabs the EMPs entered the room after the plenary meeting on the invasion of Iraq was over. The discussion revolved around technological development, and the political and economic framework required to have CCS plants built in Europe.

The breakthrough

What Bellona did not realize at the time was that the European Commission had started stepping up its work on energy and climate policy internally. One of its initiatives was to establish so-called technology platforms in which they collected all interested parties involved in every single field of technology. Industry, research, finance and civil society met here to come up with joint advice for the Commission on the way forward for sustainable technological development. The Commission's idea was to put them all in the same room and give them an opportunity to arrive at their own recommendations as to what the EU cooperation should do. One year after Bellona's hearing on "The Road to the Hydrogen Society" the Commission set aside 1 million euro to pay for a secretariat that would set up a technology platform for CCS, called the "EU technology platform of zero emission fossil fuel power plants", abbreviated to ZEP. At the same time, the Commission announced an invitation to nominate candidates to take part in the platform. A little over 40 representatives from all large energy, petroleum, research and environmental organizations were finally picked. Bellona was invited to take part together with Greenpeace, WWF, CAN-Europe and the British E3G. Industry was the dominant group with participants from all the big petroleum companies like Shell, BP, Statoil, Total, Chevron, electricity producers like the German companies E.ON and RWE, the French EDF, the Swedish Vattenfall, and the equipment suppliers Mitsui, Siemens, Alstom and General Electric. In addition, the top universities and research institutions were represented. ZEP was one of 32 technology platforms set up by the Commission in the 2000s. Together with Statoil, Bellona was the only Norwegian participant on the executive board of ZEP. At the suggestion of Bellona, both SINTEF and Aker Clean Carbon later joined the board.

Like most EU meetings, those at ZEP were very long and often complex. In the beginning the discussions were dominated by contributions from the German coal power producers, who thought CCS could only be brought to market *after* more efficient turbines had been researched, developed and installed – turbines that generated more energy per unit of fossil fuel and with lower CO_2 emissions, because the greater the efficiency of a power station, the less CO_2 and other toxic gases it emits. To our great surprise the big European electricity producers were not particularly interested in constructing CCS plants until after 2030. They viewed CCS as an extra cost and preferred to carry on business as usual, i.e. stick to the EU's quota system without taking on the heavy investments involved in purifying CO_2. The petroleum companies took a different view, however, since they wished to use CO_2 to squeeze more oil and gas out of the existing reservoirs. One of the hugely contentious issues among the participants in ZEP, therefore, was *when* they would be in a position to build demonstration plants and when CCS technology could be installed at all new power plants. Turbine suppliers, like Alstom, Siemens and General Electric, could not agree either. Siemens were reticent, clearly, and adopted the same approach as their customers at the power companies, seeing no hurry to develop the technology before 2020. Alstom, on the other hand, thought the problem was not a lack of technology but a lack of market confidence in CCS's ability to work and be commercially profitable.

After two years' negotiations, mostly in working parties within each field of CCS's value chain, ZEP concluded that the technology could become commercially viable from 2020 if a European quota system for CO_2 emissions was put in place, making the cost about 30-45 euro per tonne of CO_2. At the same time, 10-12 full-scale demonstration plants had to be built, which would contribute to industrializing the capture technology and thus bring down the price per tonne of CO_2 captured, transported and stored. The Commission took part in the majority of the ZEP meetings, also at working party level. It transpired that Bellona's representatives were at the very forefront in their understanding of the technology and instrumentation. Participating alongside Frederic Hauge, who was elected vice-chairman of ZEP's executive board early on, were Aage Stangeland, with a doctorate in materials engineering from SINTEF (the Foundation for Scientific and Industrial Research at the Norwegian Institute of Technology (NTH)), Marius Holm, Beate Kristiansen with experience from Statoil's CO_2 storage project at Sleipner, and senior information officer Anne-Karin Sæther and myself with experience from the EU's political processes. All the representatives from Bellona took an active part in the debate, and Bellona was quickly voted into the executive group of several central working parties. Being top-heavy on participating engineers in the working parties, however, it made the written material rather inaccessible. CCS is comparable to rocket science, i.e. complicated, as it consists of several highly engineered solutions. McKinsey & Co were hired in to oversee the work on the political strategy memorandum. But even the able consultants had to resort to a copywriter of their own. British Hermione St. Leger had no prior knowledge of CCS, but a good ability to listen and formulate the most important messages in readily understandable fashion. She was invaluable in the work to craft a comprehensible message based on the broad-based and technical participation from various countries and cultures.

After two years ZEP delivered a detailed report on the need for framework conditions in research, economy and regulatory matters. The report established that, technically, CCS was altogether possible in terms of both the capture, transport and storage of CO_2. The main challenge lay in scaling up the technology, i.e. building demonstration plants with the capacity to capture CO_2 from large power plants, from 250 MW upwards. At the same time, the report stressed the need to get started on large-scale storage of CO_2 in order to reassure the sceptics that storing the greenhouse gas underground in deep-lying geological formations is a safe proposition. Financial incentives were proposed, in the form of both subsidy schemes to build the first 10-12 large demonstration plants and a higher price for emitting CO_2 once testing of the technology had been completed.

The results from ZEP and other technology platforms were collected by the Commission and presented to the EU countries' energy ministers, and later their heads of state. At a summit meeting in March 2007 Angela Merkel announced the EU's energy and climate strategy up to 2020, better known as "The 2020 Package". In it the EU's heads of state undertook to reduce greenhouse gas emissions by 20 percent by 2020. The heads of state asked the Commission to table within one year a legislative proposal on emission quota trading, an increase in renewable energy sources, energy efficiency measures and CCS technology development. In the communication, the EU's heads of state pointed specifically to the need to create regulations for storing CO_2 underground and constructing 10-12 demonstration plants by 2020. No one had expected such a detailed reference to the work at ZEP.

The communication from the EU's senior executives was given a good reception by the CCS milieu. Nevertheless, there were great challenges involved in sourcing the money for the 10-12 CCS projects. ZEP, therefore, quickly focused its searchlight on how the EU countries could fund such large and costly demonstration plants. Norway had already announced financing of a test installation with a full-scale CCS plant to follow at Mongstad, while the EU countries would soon find themselves on the sharp end of the biggest financial crisis since the Second World War. The idea of earmarking 4-6 billion euro of the EU's budget to test CCS technology was virtually a pipedream now that the financial crisis was forcing large cutbacks in national budgets.

Together with a group of financiers, led by the British organization Climate Change Capital, Bellona took part in the development of a financing instrument to pay for the big demonstration plants. The gist of the plan was to use the EU's quota trading directive or Emissions Trading System (ETS) by earmarking the income from auctioning emission quotas to build CCS plants. When companies need more emission permits than they have been allocated, they go onto the market to buy extra quotas. They can either be purchased from the government or from companies that have invested in environmental engineering and no longer need the quotas they have received. The revenue from the authorities' sales of emission quotas goes straight into the state coffers and represents a large and significant source of income for many countries with economic problems. Consequently, the proposal was pretty unpopular among the governments of the EU's member states.

The scheme became the object of intense lobbying activity in autumn 2008. The European Climate Foundation (ECF) got involved in the work, also providing the funding to coordinate lobbying with the European Parliament and the EU member states for the environmental organizations. Its own ad hoc network, CCS Leadership Forum, was created, made up of industrialists, geologists, and research and environmental organizations. First the members of the EU Parliament's Committee on Environment had to agree to the proposal. The Conservative Irish MEP Avril Doyle was rapporteur for the EU's Emission Trading Scheme Directive trading directive. She found the proposal interesting, along with the enthusiastic help by MEP Chris Davies from the UK's Liberal Party , they put forward a corresponding amendment. Then, one by one, representatives were called upon to present the concept and the vision behind the financing scheme. And it was not uncommon for us to be queuing in the corridor outside the EMPs' office waiting to get in and explain the proposal.

The Commission, conversely, was strongly opposed to the idea of using income from the sale of CO_2 quotas to finance one specific climate technology. Stavros Dimas, the Greek Commissioner for Environment, was not a great fan of CCS either. Greece has no geological formations able to store CO_2 and the technology was completely unfamiliar to him. The vote on the European Parliament's Committee on Environment took place on Thursday, 7 October 2008. It was barely three weeks after the Lehman Brothers were declared bankrupt in New York, and panic had begun to spread on the international finance market. The first time the proposal was put to the vote, it was defeated by a handful of votes. When it was voted down for a second time because there was a so-called compromise proposal, Jerzy Buzek – former Polish Prime Minister and later President of the European Parliament – rose to his feet and reiterated the importance of the proposal to enable the countries of Eastern Europe to continue using their own energy sources and not have to be dependent on Russian gas. To everyone's great surprise the proposal was passed by a good margin. Only then did the representatives of the Commission understand the severity of the matter. With that clear vote on the Parliament's Committee on Environment, nicknamed "NER 300",[1] the proposal looked assured of a majority when it came to

---

[1]   NER 300 stands for New Entrants Reserves, 300 million.

the plenary vote a couple of months later. The "NER 300" scheme was becoming a reality. The following day, in bold type, the *Financial Times* announced that the European Parliament had earmarked 9-12 billion euro to fund CCS.[2]

It was now up to the EU's Council of Ministers to rule on the case, and here there was great opposition. The French Minister for Environment and Energy, who had presidency of the EU, called the scheme "the biggest daylight robbery going", since the money that belonged to the member states' treasuries was to be channelled straight into the CCS projects and hence into the pockets of industry. That was not easy to swallow, especially for countries like Greece and Germany, which did not want demonstration plants and owing to the financial crisis were in dire need of income for the state purse. Negotiations on the EU's Council of Ministers were set to become even more thorny when countries like Sweden, Austria and Poland opposed "NER 300" too. In an attempt to gain acceptance from the opponents, the French presidency therefore descended to a much lower level. Sweden and Austria, which were sceptical about CCS, joined forces to propose that the scheme also be made applicable to renewable energy projects that were far off the commercialization stage.

At the EU summit on 12 December 2008 the matter of "NER 300" was left right till the end of the meeting. It was to be an unusually dramatic and exciting summit meeting. The EU's reaction to the tense situation between Georgia and Russia after the Russian occupation of parts of Georgia, and how the EU should tackle what was to be the start of the financial crisis, topped the agenda. In addition, the EU leaders were set to adopt the controversial energy and climate package. The French President, Nicolas Sarkozy, had already left the meeting to present the headline news to the press about fresh progress in the EU's defence and foreign-policy cooperation, the 200 million euros economic rescue package, and agreement on the EU's new energy and climate strategy. All the players in the "CCS leadership" coalition were kept posted about the negotiations by texts from the British delegation. Great was the disappointment when Parliament's proposal of 500 million quotas was reduced to 100 million by the French presidency.

---

[2]   300 million emission quotas priced at 30 euro was equivalent to 9 billion euro.

A hundred million quotas would not be enough to demonstrate the different types of capture and storage methods for CO_2. It was then that the British showed their splendid aptitude for negotiating tactics. During negotiations at such meetings, three things count: going on the offensive, showing willing to give to other countries and ensuring that one immediately has backing for the next contribution to the debate. The British special representative for climate change, John Ashton, who also took part in Great Britain's delegation to the EU summit, recorded the following speaking note for Prime Minister Gordon Brown: the EU is obliged to contribute to the G8 countries' commitments to build 20 full-scale CCS plants globally by 2020. The reference to the G8 neutralized all resistance from the Italian Prime Minister, Silvio Berlusconi. He himself often alluded to meetings with colleagues at the G8 meetings because he knew it impressed his other colleagues from the small EU countries. The NER scheme had also been expanded to pay for projects in EU countries with renewable technology. Therefore, the British proposed increasing the scheme to 300 million quotas. That placated Austria and Sweden and gave the Greeks some hope of extra economic aid, and consequently these countries no longer opposed the proposal. As agreed, the Dutch Prime Minister followed this up immediately, emphasizing the role of CCS technology in safeguarding the future value of the gas resources in the North Sea. The Danes could not gainsay that, sharing the Shelf with the Netherlands and Germany, even though their officials had been sceptical of CCS owing to popular resistance to CO_2 storage. The Dutch contribution provided the positive mood needed and meant that the French presidency was able to look at the clock and say: "I believe we have an acceptable compromise." At that late point in the afternoon, no one wanted to flex political muscle to change the mood. The Frenchman looked around and banged his gavel on the desk. "NER 300" was unanimously adopted by the EU's executives. We were able to breathe a sigh of relief.

In the agreement between the Council and Parliament the Commission was designated to finalize the details of how to distribute the money raised by auctioning the 300 million emission quotas. The Commission spent a year and a half reaching agreement with the member states as to how to share out the money, partly because Germany was having a go at retaliation and wanted money earmarked for each country based on the size of its economy. That was not to be. But the criteria for being awarded support became so lengthy that many CCS projects fell by the wayside. In addition, the price of the quotas fell drastically, reducing the size of the funding apportioned. In March 2008, when the "NER 300" proposal was carved out, the price of an emission quota stood at 32 euro. (That is to say more than 9.6 billion euro for CCS.) In December 2012, when the emission quotas were sold, they fetched 4.5 euro. In the process, the value of the funding scheme had dropped from over 9.6 billion to 1.2 billion euro. The entire support scheme plummeted in value and removed the vital economic support for the costly technology.

On 18 December 2012, four years after the scheme was adopted by the European Council, Commissioner for Climate Action Connie Hedegaard announced that "NER 300" was a milestone in the EU's climate policy that had generated 2 billion euro in private investments to match the Commission's 1.2 billion euro. Twenty-three projects in 14 EU countries with energy production from biomass, concentrated solar power, sea and wind together received 3.2 billion euro from the Commission, the member states and the companies themselves. "This confirms the EU's position as the frontrunner in the production of renewable energy and will create jobs in the EU right now", stated a proud Connie Hedegaard during the Commission's press conference.[3]

No full-scale CCS plant has yet seen the light of day in Europe. Only the Canadians have managed to build a full-scale plant in Saskatchewan, which was opened in October 2014. A British plant, White Rose, received a subsidy from "NER 300" in 2014 but was later abandoned. The EU will not reach its objective of building 10-12 plants by 2020. The technology is at an extremely critical stage. The EU's climate targets for 2050 cannot be met without CCS. Particularly for decarbonising industry. More and more politicians are starting to grasp this; and with the spotlight on cutting imports of Russian gas to Eastern Europe, the importance of energy based on burning coal, with CCS, is now emerging. All hope is not lost, therefore, that CCS can become a reality in Europe.

---

[3] A. Reece, "No winner found in EC's CCS competition", *Resource*, 18 December 2012.

Norway, the land of post hoc

Norwegian players were not able to take part in the first round of the "NER 300" scheme, which is to say that they were unable to make use of the EU's funding of CCS and renewable projects. The reason was that the quota trading directive, of which the scheme was part, had not been included in the EEA Agreement. Statoil had informed the Norwegian Ministry of Petroleum and Energy that the company did not envisage using "NER 300", because they regarded the chances of the EU countries agreeing on the scheme with the Parliament as very slight.[4] The mood subsequently changed. Norway and DG Climate agreed that Norwegian players could take part in the second and last round after all once the procedures had all been completed and the directive had become part of the EEA Agreement. All the EU countries arranged their own seminars on how to go about applying to the "NER 300" programme. Even the authorities in little Malta held a whole-day seminar to provide information on procedures and documentation requirements for Maltese applicants. On the Ministry of Petroleum and Energy's webpage a short press release was published to the effect that Enova would handle applications for the subsidization of renewable energy, and the ministry itself was dealing with CCS projects.[5] When a call was made to the person in charge at Enova to ask when they were planning a briefing meeting, given that the time for submission of applications was supposedly very short, the people in charge at Enova replied "We have no plans for any seminar. We know all the potential candidates".[6] The Ministry of Petroleum and Energy had no plans to inform the Norwegian CCS community either, but received a project application from the Norwegian company Sargas, which the ministry later rejected.[7] Then, in a press release, the Minister of Petroleum and Energy, Ola Borten Moe, stated that the ministry would not send the application on to the Commission because the project was not up

---

[4]   Conversation with Hydro's and Statoil's representatives in Brussels, autumn 2008.
[5]   Ministry of Petroleum and Energy (OED's) website, 3 April 2013.
[6]   Phone conversation with Rune Holmen, officer in charge of case at Enova, May 2013.
[7]   It was The Brussels office, where I was Chairman of the Board, that wrote the application on behalf of the Norwegian company.

to scratch. He later told *Dagens Næringsli*[8] that the ministry felt that forwarding the application to the Commission would obligate the ministry to pay 50 percent of the expenses if it were to pass through the eye of the Commission's needle. That was incorrect, as the question of co-funding by the authorities would only be relevant if the project was pre-approved by the Commission. Clearly, Ola Borten Moe had not studied the protocol and procedures of the "NER 300" scheme well enough. It would also have been ignominious for him if the EU had had to finance a Norwegian CCS project while the government's own moon landing project at Mongstad was at a standstill. Norwegian CCS players, from the equipment and petroleum industry to research environments and mainland industry, thus missed out on hundreds of millions of euro's worth of possible support because the Norwegian government put its biased attitude towards the EU ahead of the possibilities offered by the EU cooperation.

At the meeting of the European Council in October 2014 the "NER 300" scheme was highlighted as the EU's most important source of funding for low-carbon technologies up to 2030. The scheme must be strengthened financially in order to be able to support European industry, renewable energy and energy efficiency measures. It may be Europe's last chance to realize CCS. For Norway, this is particularly important because it can extend exports of Norwegian gas to Europe and ensure that Norway and Europe can hit the UN's climate targets.

---

[8]   *Dagens Næringsliv*, 12 July 2013.

CHAPTER 7

With Our Backs to the World

Crises and conflicts continue to dog Europe after the financial crisis. Low economic growth, high unemployment, and the energy and climate conflict mean that new methods of solving problems are in the pipeline. The EU cooperation faces sweeping changes that Europe has not seen since incorporating the countries of Central and Eastern Europe in 2004. Norway must come to terms with this, on the inside or on the outside.

A Europe in crisis

The EU cooperation of the 2010s is characterized by abortive economic policy that has produced intolerably high unemployment and social unrest. 24.6 million people were unemployed in the EU in August 2014. It is little comfort that this is a fall of 1.7 million from 2013.[1] In Greece youth unemployment is far above 50 percent, and there is talk of a lost generation. The same goes for Spain, although the figure for young people neither working nor studying is about 25 percent, as indeed Sweden would also have experienced if young Swedes had not been able to come to Norway to work. This is a very grave situation, as a result of which the EU cooperation is currently facing its biggest crisis since its start-up after the Second World War.

The EU's position in society suffers from an inability to engage people and take decisions that people understand, popularly called the "democratic deficit". Furthermore, the low rate of support for the elections to the European Parliament attest to the fact that the Parliament and the EU's role are not reaching out to people adequately. At the time of the last parliamentary elections in May 2014, election turnout

---

[1]   Unemployment statistics, Eurostat, August 2014.

was about 43 percent. The response varied by countries: 57.22 percent in Italy, 51.7 percent in Sweden, 33.67 percent in Portugal and 13.05 percent in Slovakia.[2] It is a clear drop from the 62 percent electoral response the first time the EU parliamentarians in nine countries stood for election in 1979. Electoral participation in all democracies is challenging. In American mid-term elections to Congress (when not a presidential election), electoral participation is barely more than 30 percent. Another important aspect is that the protest parties, whether from the extreme right or the extreme left, have benefited from the European Parliament elections, as they did at the last election in May 2014. Both sides of the political spectrum wish to return to a Europe of nation-states, with closed borders, trading just in traditional goods. In countries like France, Great Britain, Austria and Denmark the anti-EU parties have made progress, netting some 130 out of a total of 751 mandates. Together they do not have the power to establish a joint group with a joint voice. Nevertheless, the parties want to be heard to a far greater degree over the next five years. If the European Parliament is to present the appearance of a democratic arena, it is healthy for all parties to have opposition to the EU project come forward and be heard in the public space. That is why the representatives sit according to party groups, not the countries they come from. Nonetheless, the EU is perceived as one single authority for those not working in societally related areas on a daily basis or sitting nearby. The reality is different, however. In the day-to-day work of the Commission's expert groups, the Council's working parties or the European Parliament's committees, the contrasts and clashes are often great, resulting in frequent confrontations. French ambitions, British pragmatism, Polish obstinacy and German interests meet in a thunderous clash every single day. The conference tables of the EU institutions are the modern-day European battlefield. The problem is that all those bloody fights are not seen. People never get to know how tough and confrontational the EU's decision-making processes are. We just get told it takes time.

The EU has become a conveniently accessible whipping boy for all problems on the continent. Many governments and heads of state in the EU countries often blame the EU when they introduce reforms they themselves have voted for in Brussels – whether expensive, technical

---

[2]   European Parliament, results of the European elections 2014.

measures like strengthening the safety of European tunnels or removing costly and competition-distorting subsidies for industry. When they have to stump up the money from national budgets to fund such measures, they blame it on "EU requirements", thereby adding more fuel to the view of the EU as a source of society's problems, not as part of the solution.

The economic difficulties in the Mediterranean countries may seem to point towards the EU being on the verge of a precipice. The economic decline in Europe with galloping unemployment and social unrest is repulsive to us. The fact that the EU is being propelled forward without the participation of Norwegian politicians only increases the gap to understanding Europe's development. Slowly but surely, a picture of *them and us* is evolving. Norwegian journalists have no one to interview, no peg on which to hang an article. Norwegian textbooks devote little attention to the EU cooperation apart from referring to Norwegian defiance and the referenda. The difference is tangible by comparison with our neighbours' textbooks, which include the history of the EU, the most important treaties, enlargements and distinctive features of all member states in the syllabus. In Belgian textbooks for fifth-grade children, it says that Norway and Switzerland do not wish to join the European cooperation because they are so affluent.

In recent years Norwegian awareness of the EU has largely homed in on individual directives in which Norwegian points of view have not been consulted. By the time the discussion finally does reach Norway, the EU institutions' negotiations have already concluded three to five years previously. Well-known examples are the Postal Directive, the Temporary Worker Directive and the Data Storage Directive. These have reinforced the view that anything coming from the EU is no good for Norway. Of the 287 legislative amendments, the *Storting* brought in as a result of the EU *acquis* during the period 1992 to 2011, 265 were adopted unanimously. Those who voted in favour include arch-EU opponents like the Norwegian Socialist Left Party (SV) and the Centre Party.[3]

---

[3]   Norwegian white paper NOU 2012: 2 Utenfor og innenfor, pp. 821-823.

EU cooperation on the wane

The past 70 years of Europe's history clearly show that cooperation between European countries has stemmed from economic and political crises and conflicts. No countries collaborate just because they are neighbours, or because it is easy. Countries collaborate because they have an interest in doing so – because they have to. It is a case of committing to binding cooperation to achieve something that could not have been accomplished alone. This applies equally to the European Union.

The European Coal and Steel Union was set up amid the ruins of the Second World War. This was the tender infancy of the EU. The EU's Single Market, with its removal of trade barriers between countries, and the EEA Agreement were measures to counter the economic crises after the oil shocks of the 1970s. The fall of the Berlin Wall and the end of the Cold War led to the historic enlargement of the EU. The Balkan Wars in the 1990s clearly showed the need to set up cooperation overseas and on defence. The financial crisis in 2008 revealed gaping holes in the Euro cooperation and on the financial market, resulting in the creation of the banking union. In 2014 new energy and foreign-policy issues surfaced when Russia annexed the Crimean Peninsula. Dramatic social conflicts in North Africa and the Middle East have led to large refugee flows arriving in Europe.

The situation experienced by Southern Europe since the financial crisis and the great social unrest in the Mediterranean countries provide a shuddering reminder of conditions during Europe's interwar period. Russian expansion in Georgia and Ukraine recall Germany's annexation of the Sudetenland in order to gather together the German-speaking peoples before the Second World War. Kate Hansen Bundt, Secretary-General of the Norwegian Atlantic Committee (DNAK), refers to the fact that Vladimir Putin has taken the relationship with the West back to 1968, when the Soviet tanks rolled into Czechoslovakia. With knowledge learned from history, the USA and the EU, together with Norway, have introduced economic sanctions against Russia. Like Stalin, Khruschchev and all their successors up to Gorbachev, Putin views voluntary cooperation between European countries as a threat to Russia's European position of strength. Putin regards Finland, Estonia, Latvia, Lithuania and the Balkan countries' wish to embed themselves within the EU and NATO, politically and economically, as a provocation to Russia. The country's behaviour has forced the EU countries to develop a common front, even though they are often miles apart in negotiations on concrete measures. The EU thus appears to be the most important arena for European security policy. NATO is no longer necessarily the natural gravitation point for Norwegian and European security.

In the 1930s Europe was fragmented. The conflicts between Germany and France had reached boiling point. In the post-war period Europe was divided into two up to the end of the Cold War. Today 28 democratic countries sit around the same table. The heads of state have chosen a Polish president, Donald Tusk, from the country that has suffered most at the hands of German-Russian rivalry over the past two hundred years. Countries like Turkey, Macedonia, Montenegro, Serbia and Albania are queuing up to join. This was the main reason for the EU being awarded the Nobel Peace Prize in 2012. It was the reason for 2,400 citizens of Oslo defying the cold winter and marching in a torchlight procession from Oslo Central Station to the Grand Hotel to display their respect for EU leaders.

For many people, the paradox is that the crisis Europe is embroiled in has accelerated EU cooperation more than curbing it. There is no doubt that the problems must be solved internationally, not nationally. As far as mutually legally binding cooperation is concerned, there are four new and extensive areas that stand out: (1) finance policy and the banking union, (2) energy, climate and the energy union, (3) economic growth through new trade agreements and (4) action to tackle the great wave of migration. All these measures are wide-ranging and will take a long time to implement, but they will all have a great bearing on Norway.

CHAPTER 8

The Banking Union

In the wake of the financial crisis and ensuing crises, the EU countries have joined forces to form a new and closer cooperation. The result is increased European solidarity, but greater discipline. It is fundamental for the Norwegian finance sector, but also a challenge for Norway.

Something no one thought possible

Until the financial crisis erupted in the USA in October 2008, a sport was being made of offering cheap loans, even to people who the banks knew would not manage to pay them off. No bank wanted to be the one that could not offer mortgages on the market. Instead the banks sold the bad loans on amongst themselves, right until they had an oversized portfolio. Some were able to be paid off eventually, but when no one was able to service the debt, the whole system cracked. When the US Department of the Treasury allowed the big investment bank Lehman Brothers to go under, the crisis was a reality, and the panic spread.

When the financial crisis hit Europe, the EU's member states responded by supplying debt-burdened banks with capital – bailing them out via central government budgets. That meant that the taxpayer had to foot the bill for the banks having taken too big risks and messing up. However, countries like Greece, Spain, Portugal and Ireland, which had already been struggling financially before the financial crisis, did not have enough money to inject enough capital into the banks. The banks dragged the countries' public finances down with them, causing them to start wobbling because they were teetering on the brink of bankruptcy. If the countries could not make capital available, the banks would collapse. People would run to the banks to secure their savings. If all bank customers take their money out at the same time – often known as a "run on the banks" – the banks soon run dry. That creates panic, as was seen after the stock exchange crash in the USA in 1929, which was the origin of the great depression.

The banking system is the veins of the economy. Without access to credit and stability on the financial market, the economy grinds to a halt. Credit is the source of economic growth for both industry and households. Debt is a gift, a source of growth and wealth, as long as it can be paid back. In 2009 many countries in Europe were on the brink of panic and bedlam. The salvation for these countries, including Greece, Spain, Portugal and Ireland, was to borrow money from the International Monetary Fund (IMF) and the other EU countries.

However, the EU's executives have turned this traditional method of rescuing banks and countries on its head over the last six years. The result of all crisis meetings in Brussels is that in the event of financial crises in future the banks will not be bailed out but "bailed in". That means that shareholders, bondholders and other private investors must take responsibility and suck up the losses if the banks take excessive risks. The banks themselves must be liable for their results, whether they operate at a profit or a loss. To the financial sector's great surprise, the EU agreed a limit on the extent of payouts to bonus schemes.[1] Thus the responsibility for future rescue actions has been shifted from the taxpayers to the banks themselves. What the EU has done is a radical restructuring of the banking system and the financial market as a whole.

One of the reasons for the crisis having such serious consequences was that a number of countries, headed by Germany, were unwilling to force the banks to settle their accounts. Angela Merkel and the German government wanted calm, above all, by protecting the banks from collapsing. Consequently, Merkel refused to transfer the losses to the lenders themselves, i.e. those who held shares in banks, government bonds and other securities.

Merkel and the other EU leaders therefore wished to build a firewall around the banks before they set about changing the ground rules. That

---

[1]   According to the EU's Capital Requirements Directive (CRD) variable remuneration for the bonuses must not exceed 100 percent of the fixed component. Variable compensation is permitted to make up to 200 percent of the fixed component, in accordance with the procedures laid down.

was why it took a disproportionately long time to put the crisis package and write-off of Greek debt in place.

If EU member states get into difficulties in future, they must be able to draw on loans to pay debt from a new European fund. They will not then have to go out onto the international finance market and run up debts to private banks.

The condition for making such a fund available is that the countries must accept having their financial control systems monitored. This will be done by means of a "customized" treaty that limits how much government debt a country can have – which the Commission is tasked with commenting and making recommendations on before central government budgets are adopted. This role is controversial because the perception is that the Commission can override a country's democratic institutions. Yet this type of audit of countries' economic policy has long been customary within the OECD. Every other year Norway and all the other OECD countries have to present their economic policy and results. They are subjected to detailed scrutiny and discussion, which is finally published in a separate report. The Commission and the EU countries will then perform the same exercise annually. The difference is that they will also have opportunities to introduce sanctions against those countries of the Eurozone that are not conducting a responsible economic policy.

In addition to strengthening coordination of the countries' economic policy, the EU has created new bodies tasked with monitoring the financial market. Regulations governing the financial market are one of the biggest areas in the EU and have always been part of the EEA Agreement. Here again the EU countries favour the introduction of supranational supervision within each of the banking, insurance and finance markets. The new EU inspectorates (or supervisor authorities) will not only have a role in coordinating national supervision but also direct authority, particularly if a crisis situation were to arise and require managing.

In the same way as in the USA, the EU's new inspectorates will monitor the countries' implementation of the new and legally binding rules intended to provide calm and stability on the financial market. This is the backdrop to, amongst others, the single deposit insurance scheme directive, where all countries must vouch for the same amount. The

EU countries wish to harmonize the amount to avoid people sending money to other countries where they will get the highest guarantee, as witnessed during the financial crisis. The directive is controversial in Norway because the government currently guarantees a value of NOK 2 million, approx. 222,220 euros. The amount throughout the EU has been fixed at 100,000 euros, approx. NOK 800,000. Following some excellent lobbying by ex-Minister of Finance Sigbjørn Johnsen, Norway has managed to negotiate a transitional scheme allowing it to retain the NOK 2 million guarantee up to 2018.

Furthermore, the Eurozone has set up a central mechanism for managing banks in crisis situations. Here it must be decided whether to close banks down or rescue them to avoid crises. Within the Eurozone, which is much more tightly knit, the European Central Bank will be made responsible for monitoring the operations of the 130 largest banks.

On balance the EU's banking union represents a pioneering new cooperation between the EU countries. Firstly, the countries make large amounts of capital available to one another; and secondly, they have transferred responsibility for governance of the banks and the financial market from national to supranational institutions. In other words, there is a combination of solidarity and collective discipline, the like of which has never been seen before. The next step is for the EU countries to give the European Central Bank authorization to issue joint government bonds for all the euro countries. In practice that will mean a transfer of debt between all the countries, to which Germany has hitherto been opposed.

The EU's new cooperation within the banking and financial sector has thrown up challenges for Norway. The EU's finance policy is one of the most comprehensive parts of the EEA Agreement. Participation in the EU's Single Market is altogether necessary to ensure the stability of the Norwegian financial market and enable the banks to compete in Europe. Even in 2013, before the EU countries agreed on the details of the new banking union, Jens Stoltenberg, then Prime Minister, travelled to Brussels to announce that Norway wished to take part in the banking union. He emphasized the need for better supervision of banks across national borders and clearly told Herman Van Rompuy, who was then President of the European Council, that Norway wished to be part of the new European fora. At the same time, Stoltenberg stressed that Norway needed its own special scheme under Section 115 of the Norwegian Constitution.

Section 115 of the Norwegian Constitution, formerly Section 93, gives the *Storting* scope to transfer authority to international organizations with a three-quarters majority. The *Storting* passed this motion in 1961, when the concept of sovereignty had a completely different meaning. A condition for the cession of sovereignty is that Norway is a full member of the organization. If Norway is not a member, the *Storting* can transfer sovereignty in areas that are "non-intrusive", which can only be interpreted as areas of little political significance. For this purpose, Section 26 of the Constitution is used, requiring just a simple majority, or 85 votes. To date Norway has joined 28 of the EU's 32 agencies, including agencies for medicines, chemicals, aviation and maritime safety and security, food safety etc. In all the agencies Norway has observer status, i.e. participation without voting rights and without the possibility of discussing political priorities, budgetary discussions or occupying executive posts. In all 28 areas, the Ministry of Justice concluded that Norwegian compliance with the agencies' authority is not in contravention of the Constitution, precisely because the agencies are not regarded as having authority of any political importance. The *Storting* has therefore made use of Section 26 of the Constitution. It is different for the financial market. The EU's newly created European system of financial supervision (ESFS) will have the option of intervening in Norwegian banks. There is a limit to what Norway can accept from an organization of which the country is not a member. This gives rise to a conflict. Section 26 cannot be used because participation in the EU's supervisory authority involves an essential cession of sovereignty. The solution will be to surrender sovereignty to EFTA's Surveillance Authority (ESA), of which we are a member, using Section 115. But ESA's role is to enforce the EU's treaties and the Commission's decisions. We are thus surrendering power to an organization that implements decisions from an organization of which we are not a member. Once again, the Norwegian people are being led down the garden path.

Even before negotiation of the EEA Agreement had been completely finalized, the EU Court of Justice ruled that the EFTA countries could not take part in the EU's decision-making bodies. The *Storting* was informed of this in 1992 before the popularly elected representatives voted in favour of Norwegian participation in the EEA. Little did the *Storting* suspect how the EU cooperation might develop in the future. The paradoxical thing is that the principle of cession of sovereignty does not apply to the Norwegian Defence, which represents Norway's safety. In Nordic Battlegroup, Norwegian soldiers are subordinate to Swedish officers and fight on behalf of the Norwegian people under the flag of the EU.

Professor Fredrik Sejersted of the University of Oslo, chairman of the Sejersted Committee (the EEA Review Committee), refers to the way Finland has solved the problem. In the first section of the Finnish constitution, it simply states that Finland "participates in international cooperation in order to promote peace and human rights and with a view to developing society".[2] It's as easy as that. For Norway, a corresponding provision will call for a decision extending over two terms of parliament.

The informal contacts

All Norwegian governments since 1994 have emphasized the use of both formal and informal contacts in dealings with the EU institutions. The public rarely gets to know who the informal contacts are. The solution to Norway's participation in the EU's new institutions for monitoring the finance market came via its own negotiations on special and differential treatment (SDT). Thanks to the Frenchman Michel Barnier, a Norwegian-friendly Internal Market Commissioner, the government has good dialogue with the Commission. Barnier once headed the French organizing committee for the Olympic Games in Albertville in 1992 and is a winter sports fan. He has been in Norway three times in past years, a record unequalled by any of his other colleagues. Each time, he has discussed the Norwegian issues with the government and central Norwegian politicians from the opposition. The important thing for Norway is that Barnier has taken the time to look at the issues from the Norwegian angle too and tried to find solutions which are legally tenable and good for both the EU and Norway. That

---

[2]   Interview with Fredrik Sejersted, "Ønsker ny EU-paragraf i Grunnloven", *Manifest tidsskrift*, 14 May 2014.

is unusual in an EU with 28 member states, where everyone is vying for attention. One essential reason for this special treatment is that the Norwegian Georg Riekeles works in Barnier's cabinet. Riekeles is the only Norwegian ever to have been employed in the cabinet of a European commissioner. His role and efforts have proved invaluable for Norway's ability to negotiate a tailor-made agreement on participation in the financial supervisory authorities. That shows how important it is to have people on the inside of the EU system. The person responsible for the EU's Single Market in the Juncker Commission from 2014 to 2019 is the Pole Elzbieta Bienkowska. The situation may then turn out differently.

The result of the negotiations on the special and differential treatment of Norway, Iceland and Liechtenstein is that EFTA's Surveillance authority (ESA) is being assigned the majority of the tasks vested in the EU's new supervisory authority. Precisely as with the EEA Agreement, in practice Norway has to relinquish authority to an organization we do not belong to. The government therefore has no choice but to go to the *Storting* and request a three-quarters majority. If they do not get it, the EU will be at liberty to demand that the whole of the EEA legislation for the financial market be removed from the agreement temporarily. That will be catastrophic for Norwegian banks and financial institutions. In all probability, therefore, even those most vehemently opposed to linking Norway to a supranational cooperation – like the Centre Party and the Norwegian Socialist Left Party (SV) – will vote for Norwegian participation. Similar new situations will arise when the EU wishes to use the same model for Norwegian participation in other new supervisory authorities and agencies like electricity, so-called ACER and NTSO-E, and the new inspection authority for electronic communications (BEREC). And if the EU's energy union were one day to become reality, an inspection authority to manage gas resources would be extremely difficult for Norway to take part in – assuming, that is, that we still have no voting rights. For the first time since 1992, Norwegian participation in the EU's financial supervisory authority will force a catholic debate in the *Storting* about Norway's relationship with the EU – and hopefully an impassioned debate countrywide.

Norway's part in the financial crisis

Norway was not spared the effects of the financial crisis in the USA and Europe. For a while the situation was perilous. Many Norwegian banks were afflicted by debt from the EU countries. The head of Norway's biggest bank, Rune Bjerke from Den Norske Bank (DNB, or DnB NOR back then) stated that the bank was in a process of decline before the government's rescue package arrived.[3] The financial market is a particularly sensitive market, where rumours and people's understanding of the crisis can lead to dramatic actions. As Bjerke put it: "The instant people press that keypad and take out their cash, it's too late."[4] If the Mediterranean countries had not managed to service their debt, Norwegian banks would have experienced panic and pandemonium too.

Norway's resilient economy and large oil assets meant that the government was able to rescue the banks overnight. The government lent Norwegian banks Norwegian kroner 350 billion, approx. 37 billion euro, without having to ask for help from either the EU or the IMF. In addition, the government was able to appropriate money on a grand scale for countercyclical measures; that is to say, projects which crash-started the economy and created new growth, such as the government's massive commitment to expanding the road network in 2010.

In order to help stabilize the debt-swamped countries of Europe, the Stoltenberg government opted to increase the Norwegian contribution to the IMF by Norwegian kroner 55 billion, approx. 6 billion euro. That was instrumental in enabling the IMF to place capital at the disposal of the EU's emergency lending institution (the European Stability Mechanism (ESM)). The government opted not to contribute to the EU's stability mechanism.

In 2012 the EU countries negotiated their way to a reduction of the Greek public debt with private creditors. All the creditors accepted the loss voluntarily, except for the National Petroleum Fund (aka the Government Pension Fund Global (SPU)), which voted against. The

---

[3]   E. Grøndahl, S. Heyerdahl and A.A. Nilsen, See http://www.nrk.no/okonomi/
gjedrem-mener-dnb-nor-var-trygg-1.7433691.
[4]   E. Grøndahl, "En kamp time for time", *NRK*, 26 Septembre 2009.

Petroleum Fund had invested Norwegian kroner 1.7 billion, approx. 181 million euros, in Greek government bonds. The reason why the Petroleum Fund voted no was that it was being treated more poorly than the European Central Bank and the European Investment Bank.

"If a company goes bankrupt, all the investors take the same loss. In the restructuring of Greece, some people were given a priority or pre-emptive right, and we're against that on principle. We make financial decisions exclusively on the basis of our long-term perspective", Yngve Slyngstad, manager of the Petroleum Fund, told *Aftenposten*.[5]

The decision was criticized by several central players in Norway. Steinar Juel, Nordea's chief economist, pointed out the lack of political thinking as the cause, while his colleague Knut Anton Mork from Handelsbanken said it was "an excellent illustration that the administration of the Petroleum Fund ought not to belong under Norges Bank".[6] The head of Attac in Norway, an international movement working towards social, environmental and democratic alternatives in the globalization process, Benedicte Pryneid Hansen, said the Petroleum Fund contributed "to undermining public welfare, and to extreme poverty development in Southern Europe".[7] Ola Storeng, financial editor of *Aftenposten*, compared the Petroleum Fund's attitude with that of "a principled debt collection agency".[8]

You could have heard a pin drop from the public gallery in Norway. As a non-member of the EU, Norway was not bound by the EU's rules on economic solidarity.

There are signs that the Greek economy is now on the mend. In any case Greece had to get a handle on its corruption, black economy and inability to collect taxes. Some reduction of its debt was unavoidable, however. If other countries and investors had reacted like Norway, the rescheduling of the Greek debt would have collapsed. Greece would probably have been pressured into leaving the Eurozone and the entire Euro cooperation might have collapsed. A new financial crisis would have swept across the world. No one can say what the consequences

---

[5]   M. Strand, "Oljefondet stemte nei til Hellas-avtalen", *Aftenposten*, 16 March 2012.
[6]   *Ibid.*
[7]   *Ibid.*
[8]   O. Storeng, *Aftenposten*, 16 March 2012.

would have been for the Norwegian economy, Norwegian jobs and Norwegian welfare. It is clear, however, that the demand for Norwegian goods and services would have declined, and the value of the Norwegian krone could have risen dramatically. Particularly onshore industry that lives off exporting to Europe would have been a casualty. With the Norwegian economy's close ties to the EU, Norway is entirely dependent on a functional European economy and calm on the financial market.

Today, the Government Pension Fund Global has recently reached approximately one trillion euro. It will certainly take a long time before Norway can come anywhere close to being in the same boat as Greece. If that day should come, however, the EU countries and private investors had better have forgotten how Bank of Norway reacted when the "debt storm" (to use George Osborne's phrase) was blowing a gale across Southern Europe in 2008-2012.

CHAPTER 9

The Energy Union

The conflicts between Russia and Ukraine have repeatedly stopped the delivery of gas to the EU. That is going to have major consequences for the EU, which relies on buying more than 50 percent of its energy from neighbouring countries. Now the EU countries want to set up their own energy union, based on the control and governance mechanisms of the banking union. The EU wants access to clean, cheap energy from reliable countries – not just to save the climate, but also to supply people with affordable electricity and build a competitive industry.

Reasonable, climate-friendly energy from home and reliable suppliers abroad

On 1 January 2009 Russia shut off the supply of gas to Ukraine. The conflict centred around an outstanding payment of 1.7 billion euro to the Russian Gazprom from the Ukrainian company Naftogaz. 8 January saw the start of a fortnight-long energy crisis in Europe because twelve EU countries had their gas supply cut off: Bulgaria, Hungary, the Czech Republic, Slovakia, Slovenia, Greece, Austria, Poland, Romania, Germany, Italy and France were without gas to varying degrees.[1] The EU then realized that it was completely and utterly dependent on Russian gas. Overnight, energy policy became the new topic of foreign policy in Brussels.

The EU imports 54 percent of all the energy used by the member states, and gas accounts for a quarter of all energy used by the EU countries. As much as 67.4 percent of the gas used by the EU is imported.[2] As of 2014

---

[1]   S. Pirani, J. Stern and K. Yafimava, *The Russo-Ukrainian Gas Dispute of January 2009: A comprehensive Assessment*, Oxford Institute for Energy Studies, February 2009, pp. 54-55.

[2]   Eurostat, "Energy Production and Imports", July 2016.

the EU countries import 35 percent of their gas from Russia. Countries like Bulgaria, the three Baltic states, Slovakia and Finland get all the gas they import from the Russians.[3] Imports from Norway have increased steadily over past years and reached the same level as Russia in 2012.[4] The last third comes from Algeria, Morocco and the Middle East. In December 2013, the European Commission presented a set of accounts showing that in 2011 the EU countries paid 420 billion euro for fossil fuel imports, a figure expected to increase by 100 billion by 2015. At the same time, sales of goods and services accounted for 400 billion.[5] Fossil energy imports give the EU a negative trade balance and represent a financial drain on the EU. In 2009 alone, a ruined Greece imported fossil fuel equivalent to 9 percent of its gross national product. At the same time, the EU's heads of state have agreed to reduce greenhouse gas emissions by between 80 and 95 percent relative to the 1990 level. This is where the EU countries have a threefold objective: to reduce their dependence on imports of gas from Russia, to shift their expenditure towards home-produced energy and energy efficiency measures, and to reduce CO_2 emissions.

The demonstrations and riots in Kiev's Maidan Square began on 23 November 2013 after the President of Ukraine, Viktor Yanukovych, refused to sign a cooperation agreement with the EU. After months of demonstrations President Yanukovych had to flee. Vladimir Putin responded by putting the price of Russian gas up by 40 percent. In February 2014 Putin embarked on annexing the Crimean Peninsula. For a country that had lived under the yoke of Soviet tyranny for 60 years, this left little doubt: now they would end their dependence on Russian gas. The EU therefore has ambitions of cutting consumption and has increased imports of natural gas sharply.

Poland is at the centre of the EU's energy and climate policy. Not only are the Poles Ukraine's neighbours, they generate practically all their energy by burning coal. Poland's dependence on coal is the same

---

[3]   A. Neslen, "Europe's Dependency on Russian Gas May Be Cut amid Energy Efficiency Focus", *The Guardian*, 9 September 2014.

[4]   G. Gotev, "Norway Overtakes Russia as EU's Biggest Gas Supplier", *Euractive*, 25 June 2013.

[5]   J. Delbeke, "EU Climate Policy: Looking Back and Looking Forward", presentation to Center for European Policy Studies (CEPS), 10 December 2013.

as Norway's dependence on hydroelectric power. Poland gets 47 percent of its gas supply for industry and other energy production from Russia through Ukraine. Poland recently entered into a contract for the supply of liquefied gas from Qatar priced closer to double the spot price in Europe. Given the combination of powerful economic growth and ageing power stations, many from the Soviet era, Poland needs to renew its energy production. In addition, Poland will one day have to pay for CO_2 emissions under the EU's quota trading directive and in line with the result of the UN's negotiations on greenhouse gas emissions in Paris in November 2015.

This places Poland at the heart of Europe's energy policy. Polish politicians, both ex-Minister of Foreign Affairs, Radoslaw Sikorski, and former President Tusk, championed the establishment of an energy union of the EU's own in April 2014. Poland wishes to see energy policy Europeanized, just like the banking union, where countries have entrusted the responsibility for overseeing the market function to the EU's own institutions. Poland wants the EU to exert its collective economic and political weight to negotiate better price terms on gas imports from countries outside the EU.

The Polish government wants the EU to pay for the construction of infrastructure to transport gas, not just to Poland but between other countries in the region.[6]

The proposal to create an independent energy union has been given a mixed reception in the EU countries. In Brussels, the majority of experts snorted at the proposal and said the EU will never be able to introduce a centralized negotiating system. The traditional view is that it is the market which negotiates and determines the price of gas, as was also stressed by ex-Commission President José Manuel Barroso and Commissioner for Energy Günther Oettinger. That is true, particularly as regards gas from Norway. As this book has shown, it was the EU that in 2001 urged Norway and the other gas-exporting EU countries to phase out centralized gas negotiations. However, those countries that have to import gas from Russia are up against a big supplier that abuses its market power: Gazprom. The EU has repeatedly called on Gazprom to open up its gas pipelines to other suppliers. That could

---

[6] "Poland calls for energy union", *Euractive*, 2 April 2014.

create competition and lower prices for European buyers. Gazprom refused to do this, and Putin is not willing to apply pressure to the company. European gas companies, but also large buyers like E.ON, RWE and Vattenfall, used to control the transportation of all gas in Europe. When the European Commission forced them to open up to deliveries from competing suppliers, the price of gas dropped by 20 percent virtually overnight. In this way, the introduction of the EU's competition rules has had a great bearing on the price level of energy and hence the competitiveness of European industry.

In Jean-Claude Juncker's Commission, one of seven vice-presidents is responsible for the energy union. That vice-president must coordinate the input from the commissioners for climate, energy, environment, research and neighbourhood relations.

Norway's views

So far, the Norwegian reaction has consisted, first and foremost, of criticizing the proposal to centralize negotiations on purchasing gas for Europe. The government has emphasized that gas is a commodity best managed with a smooth-functioning market. As long as Norway is part of the Single Market and implements all EU energy market legislation, there is very little to suggest that Norway will be covered by the centralized EU negotiations with other countries. These are meant for Russia and countries that collude to manipulate the market to keep prices up. Norway's best argument against centralizing the EU's gas negotiations, therefore, will be to implement the EU directives lined up in the EEA Agreement, the so-called third energy package. That will ensure closer cooperation between energy suppliers and distributors.

Two new EU institutions for operators and regulators of the electricity market will also become part of the EU's energy union. Both organizations have a supranational decision-making process and have the authority to coordinate and plan expansion of the power grid across national borders. In 2009 the Nordic cooperation in this field was placed under the EU. Parts of Norway's Water Resources and Energy Directorate's tasks will thus be transferred to the new EU agencies. That may also be in violation of Section 115 of the Norwegian Constitution because, as an EEA country, Norway cannot become a full member, only participate as an observer, without voting rights.

If the EU sets up the same administrative bodies for the supply and distribution of gas as for electricity, she may have a big challenge on her hands. Once again, the government will definitely have to go to the *Storting* to request a three-quarters majority to approve Norwegian participation. Furthermore, the glaring discrepancies between the EU's gas-importing countries and Norway will be thrown into even starker relief in the new institutions. To a great extent the EU will be able to lay down important terms governing the way Norwegian gas is sold and distributed in Europe.

One example of the clashes between the EU and Norway in this area is the EU's commitment to adopting energy efficiency measures and the Norwegian desire to increase gas exports. It is said that for every percent the EU succeeds in reducing energy consumption by, the demand for gas is reduced by 2.5 percent. The EU's draft directive, outlining a 30 percent improvement in energy efficiency by 2030, will therefore have great consequences for Norwegian gas exports. The Norwegian government has claimed that it will cost the EU less to increase imports of gas by switching from coal to gas than to invest in expensive efficiency improvement measures.[7]

For the EU countries increased gas imports will exacerbate the situation on several fronts. They will make the EU more dependent on imports from Russia and other countries with unstable political regimes. They will also increase the EU's trade balance deficit because they do not benefit the EU's own economy. Preparing to buy more gas, therefore, contributes neither to energy security, economic growth, industry nor employment.

The EU's climate targets for 2030 will also be an integral part of the energy union. Norway assumed the EU's objectives for 2020 and as an EEA country will have to adopt a position on the new policy for 2030. The ambitions are clear: a 40 percent reduction in CO_2 emissions in 2030 as compared to the 1990 level. This will be achieved by tightening up trading in CO_2 quotas, increasing the proportion of renewable

---

[7]   Norwegian government, "Norwegian position on the proposed EU framework for climate and energy policies towards 2030".

energy to 27 percent and reducing energy consumption by 27 percent. In Norway, the objective of a greater proportion of renewable energy will be met with scepticism by the hydroelectric power producers. Norway is therefore banking on the EU's new renewable targets not being made legally binding for every country, as is the case with the 2020 targets. Norwegian hydroelectric power producers fear lower electricity prices, and hence lost profits, due to the glut of energy on the market. This can only be solved by laying enough cables from Norway to the continent. In that case Norwegian hydroelectric power can also act as a green battery for parts of Northern Europe: When the sun sets and the wind subsides on the continent, Norway can transmit hydroelectrically generated electricity. Conversely, when the sun rises, the power will be sent back and stored in hydropower reservoirs. The Commission's proposal on trading CO_2 emission quotas says that all countries must make emission reductions within the EU and in their own country. That will be a big challenge for Norway, which is gearing up to buy climate quotas in developing countries. Those cuts which Norway cannot handle at home, mainly due to the petroleum sector, will be made in other countries by means of payment. This mechanism has been entirely legitimate under the Kyoto Agreement. The EU's 2030 energy and climate package also paves the way for a new control mechanism in which countries in the same region will enter into closer cooperation to coordinate the production and distribution of energy. Norwegian participation in this control mechanism will be extremely important in order for Norway to export power and avoid accumulating power in Norway, with attendant low prices for its energy producers. Setting up the EU's energy union will be a milestone in the history of the EU cooperation. But the new union is still on the drawing board. The EU, and Norway – as Europe's largest energy nation – have everything to gain from Norway taking part in shaping the look of a future energy union. If we do not do so, a crossroads may appear in Norway's relationship with our neighbours.

CHAPTER 10

The EEA Across the Atlantic

The EU countries, together with US President Barack Obama, have launched negotiations on a new and trail-blazing partnership for trade and investment between the USA and the EU. The agreement will be like a big EEA Agreement, with the exception of work permits. It involves removing customs on goods and services, market access with protection of investors and access to public procurement. The agreement may mean great opportunities and readjustments for Norwegian business, The election of President Trump has put the negotiations on hold.

The World Trade Organization (WTO) is at a deadlock. After the large-scale unrest in Seattle in 1999, the new round of negotiations, called the Doha Round, did not get underway until 2001. As of today, the WTO countries have failed to reach agreement in the Doha Round, which is now being negotiated for the 13th year. What is more, the American and European economies are battling low growth figures and high unemployment. Within the framework of WTO cooperation, agreements on special trade terms are being concluded between national regions. The USA and the EU therefore proposed negotiating a new agreement, called the Transatlantic Trade and Investment Partnership (TTIP), though the agreement is referred to as being between the EU and the USA in the Norwegian version.

In the USA customs duty on Norwegian products is generally low. The level is about 3-5 percent. Many products have 25 percent, such as special-purpose vehicles, or up to 100 percent, as with silicon for solar panels. If the trade agreement between the EU and the USA eliminates customs duty on products from the EU countries to the USA, it will be a substantial handicap for Norwegian competitors nonetheless.

Thanks to the EEA Agreement there are no customs on goods destined for the EU except for fish and agricultural produce, which are not covered by the agreement. If the EU and the USA reduce customs on trade in fish, Norwegian fish exporters will again be left alone with customs barriers on exports to both the EU and the USA. Their competitive situation will then be worsened considerably. Norway exports few agricultural products to the USA and the EU.

If TTIP succeeds, then firstly it will open up the American market to public procurement. Exactly as in the EU and the EEA today, competitors from the USA will be able to take part in public bidding rounds in Europe and vice versa. This is a potentially large market for the Norwegian construction industry, architects' firms, shipping, the finance industry and other service industries. Norwegian players will not reap the benefit of this opening-up of the USA market unless Norway enters into an agreement of its own or becomes part of TTIP.

TTIP's other main area is regulation and standards. Anyone who has tried to import a car from the USA to Norway will know how many technical differences there are. Just as with the "Cassis de Dijon" ruling, which eliminated all unnecessary trade barriers, the intended purpose of TTIP is to change the procedures for approving technical standards between the USA and the EU. This is one of the controversial parts of the agreement.

Many fear that low American standards will demolish the EU's regulatory framework governing health, safety and the environment. However, it is worth noting here that the USA has far stricter rules than the EU in many areas. For example, there are practically no diesel vehicles in the USA. Only 2.8 percent of passenger cars in the USA run on diesel, while that proportion is well over 50 percent in Europe[1] – not because petrol is so cheap but owing to the American authorities' strict requirements on NO_x and particulate emissions. In other areas, the reverse is true. Here an evaluation will have to be made on a field-by-field basis.

The third area involves ground rules for those areas closely connected with trade. The EU and the USA must respect each other's rules for protecting investments, competition legislation and government subsidies. This is the backdrop to the controversial proposal to set up a dispute resolution mechanism between companies and authorities

---

[1]   M. Rocco, "Can Diesel Cars Make Inroads in America", *Fox Business*, (figures of HIS Automotive), 15 July 2014.

(*Investor-State Dispute Settlement* (ISDS)). Such a mechanism will give companies a channel for suing authorities outside the national courts. At the European Parliament and the European Consumer Organization (BEUC) there is great opposition to including such a dispute resolution mechanism. Germany has also come out with strong reservations about including ISDS in TTIP. The source of the fear is that plentifully resourced multinationals will be able to take authorities to court to demand compensation for lost earnings. Over the past 15 years investors have increasingly made use of the possibility of demanding financial compensation via their own dispute resolution mechanisms that operate outside of the national judicial authorities.

Currently, 1,400 different such agreements exist between the EU countries and third countries – the term used by the EU system to denote non-member states. The tobacco company Philip Morris has sued the authorities in Uruguay for 2 million dollars in lost earnings owing to the country's requirement to label its cigarette packets with a health warning. Philip Morris did that in Norway too, but the requirement was dismissed by the EFTA Court. Vattenfall has done likewise in Germany after the Merkel government agreed to close down the company's nuclear power plant. Critics of ISDS claim that only threats of such legal action will have a demotivating effect on the authorities 'wish to introduce rules that protect health and the environment. Thus, the scheme acts as a threat to democratic processes for developing and adopting legislation. Others claim that precisely because of various countries' agreements in this field TTIP has to put in place a fairer and more predictable way of resolving conflicts. The scheme is then expected to provide greater security for investors, which will increase investments, contribute to economic growth and create more badly needed jobs.

If the EU and the USA succeed in negotiating TTIP, it will entail great potential and wide-ranging consequences for, amongst others, the iron silicide industry in North Norway and Norwegian fish and livestock farming. Other examples are trade in raw materials like petroleum products and minerals. Shipping services between American ports are only allowed for vessels owned, operated and built in the USA and by American manpower, under the controversial American Jones Act. If the EU does manage to prize apart the protected shipping sector, it will unleash a historic opportunity for the Norwegian shipping and offshore industry.

If Norway is going to affiliate itself with TTIP, this will be subject to approval by both the USA and the EU. One alternative is for Norway to negotiate its way to a parallel agreement with the USA, in which case it will complicate the EEA Agreement, because goods within EEA areas can be traded freely between countries.

It is unrealistic to think that Norway can take part in *just some* parts of TTIP. Such agreements are negotiated on the basis of an appreciation of a balanced solution, in which some sectors give and others take. In practice that means the parties agreeing on "all or nothing". If the Americans let Norwegian shipping services in, they will most certainly demand access to Norwegian markets for other sectors, for example food. This is the context in which the EU's dismantling of tariffs on food and agricultural produce will very likely be applied to Norway too. As this book has shown, Norwegian food and agricultural interests have represented the lion's share of the Norwegian opposition to a customs union, and to supranational cooperation in Scandinavia, the Nordic region and Europe. Every time our neighbours have taken the initiative to embark on cooperation in the field of agriculture and food, Norway has succeeded in keeping these sectors outside the agreements. TTIP can change this. The agreement may bring with it considerable requirements for the Norwegian farming and food industry in terms of adapting if the parties arrive at a reduction in existing trade barriers. The Federation of Norwegian Agricultural Co-operatives (FNAC) has already begun to lobby intensely against Norwegian participation in TTIP. It is worth noting that NHO seems to be split in its take on TTIP. On the one hand NHO is arguing strongly for increased trade as the engine driving economic growth. On the other hand, that enthusiasm is played down considerably when it comes to the food industry. Here NHO is talking about the need for closer dialogue and contact.[2] The board of *NHO Mat og Drikke* (FoodDrinkNorway) is made up of Orkla and other producers of ice-cream, jam and spreads, i.e. products that are currently protected by Protocol 3 of the EEA Agreement. The dairy producer

---

[2]   Comment from NHO during the European Movement's seminar on TTIP during Arendalsuken, a week-long informal meeting between politicians and businessmen, in 2014.

Tine is also part of NHO and has long fought against competition from European companies like Danone.

Nowadays a Norway outside the EU can enjoy only a spectator's view as TTIP develops. The Solberg government has claimed that Norway will have greater access to information from the USA than from the EU.[3] All EU negotiating positions, however, are cleared in advance by all the member states and in consultation with the European Parliament. That means that access to information about TTIP should be no different to Norway's access to information about other areas of EU policy. The great difference from last time the EU took the initiative for an agreement of the same dimensions, namely the EEA, is that Norway was then one of several countries of great economic and strategic importance to the EU. As a result, Norway joined in with the development of the Single Market as an EEA member *before* the Single Market came into force. That is not the case today. Today Norway and our two EFTA partners are of no strategic importance to the EU. We have to admit that in all honesty. Unlike the European Commission's former leader, Jacques Delors, the present Commission President, Jean-Claude Juncker, is not particularly concerned about the EFTA countries. Norway therefore depends on goodwill from both the EU and the USA. The last time the EU took the initiative for a united European market, it resulted in an EEA in which Norway emerged as a clear winner. Norwegian participation in TTIP can be equally significant. The TTIP negotiators envisage added value equivalent to 120 billion euro for the EU and 95 billion euro for the USA.[4] If those forecasts are as spot-on as the forecasts projected for the EU's Single Market, TTIP may well prove to be extremely useful for Norway as well. Just as things were destined to turn out with the EEA, the agreement with the USA could help fuel a revival in Norwegian industry, commerce and trade. TTIP will give small, open economies like Norway access to a bigger market on a par with its competitors. Few countries are better placed than Norway to benefit from the possibilities and tackle the readjustments.

---

[3] V. Helgesen, "Sendt på gangen", *Dagbladet*, 19 July 2014.

[4] Carnegie Europe, "Is TTIP a strategic issue", 8 October 2014.

CHAPTER 11

Migration Policy

While Europe's economic growth has stagnated in parts, the continent looks entirely different to refugees from the world's conflict-ridden regions. Fairness and solidarity in burden-sharing internationally dictate that Europe take its share of the responsibility for the world's refugees.

The Arab spring reaches Europe

After the Arab Spring in 2011 a colossal number of refugees gambled on the perilous escape from North Africa across the Mediterranean to Europe. The civil war in Syria and Libya is causing the flow of refugees to increase steadily. The conflicts in Sudan, Somalia and Eritrea are profound and show few signs of a solution. Figures from the International Organization for Migration show that 3,000 refugees perished from exhaustion or drowning while crossing the Mediterranean in the first nine months of 2014 alone.[1] Since 2000 the number of fatalities has reached no less than 22,394. That is more than half of refugee deaths for the whole world in the same period.[2] Europe is destination number one, but also the most hazardous place to travel to. Escaping across the Mediterranean is often nothing but people-smuggling, with individuals paying thousands of euro for false identity papers to get an entry clearance certificate. When 368 refugees drowned off the Italian island of Lampedusa, furthest out into the Mediterranean, in October 2013, the powerful TV images circled the entire globe and created big headlines here in Norway and in the European media. But it went quiet after that. Italy mounted a humanitarian operation of its own, *Mare*

---

[1] International Organization for Migration, "Tragedy at Sea in Lampedusa: One Year On", press release, 3 October 2014.

[2] According to IOM 40,000 refugees died from 2000 to 2013, making Europe clearly the most dangerous destination for people fleeing.

Nostrum, but is now saying that the country cannot afford to carry on the work, which has cost 9 million euro a month. So far the EU has set up Frontex, joint patrolling of all external borders with the Schengen countries, in which Norway is taking part with both its skills and resources. However, the patrol has neither the capacity nor the authority to rescue refugees making their way across the Mediterranean. The EU countries have therefore set up Triton, a support function tasked with performing the humanitarian missions.

As a great shipping nation, Norway has a number of vessels in the area. Norwegian vessels often run across refugees in emergencies. The Norwegian ships Siem Pilot and Peter Henry von Koss have saved approximately 60,000 refugees during the two years they have been part of Frontex. However, they do not have the capacity to tackle the ever mounting number of destitute and distressed people at sea.

Europe cannot open its doors wide open, particularly given the economic crisis and the political climate. Lack of integration capacity and increased pressure on welfare benefits are weighing society down. In many countries, powerful xenophobic political forces are springing up. However, Europe cannot close its doors and run away from universally forged rights like the right to political asylum for people fleeing from war and violence. That would be turning our backs on European values and traditions. After all, Norway and the other countries of Western Europe did take in refugees running from dictatorships and oppression on our own continent. This is a serious dilemma that is colouring political discussions in every country.

Within the EU an independent cooperation has been set up, the Dublin Agreement, which Norway has also endorsed. It is intended to prevent secondary waves of asylum seekers. The guiding principle is that asylum seekers must have their applications processed in the country they come to first. The Mediterranean countries, the first port of call on the journey to other European countries, have a weak economy and do not have the capacity to give refugees the treatment they are entitled to. Those coming to Northern Europe are often refugees with considerable resources or skill-sets who can make themselves useful on the labour market. The EU's migration policy does not have the authority to determine which and how many refugees each country should admit, but cooperation has joint rules concerning the way people are to be received and assessed. The problem is that the EU's migration and asylum policy does not include any mechanism for distributing the burden of asylum seekers. On the contrary, those who have found their way up to countries like Norway unlawfully are sent back to the country they first arrived at. Countries like Greece, Italy and Spain then get fresh refugees from the south and return consignments of old refugees from the north. Some of the EEA money from Norway is therefore spent on expanding Greek reception capacity.

The large global streams of people on the run have put existing international conventions under pressure. The UN track and traditional forms of cooperation are not up to tackling the problems being faced: They do not have supranational forms of decision-making and lack enforcement capabilities. Sooner or later new forms of cooperation that can distribute burdens and responsibilities in an effective and economically fair way will force their way into the open. How and when those new initiatives will see the light of day is not easy to prophesy. Nonetheless, it is apparent that the EU has to find new solutions and forms of cooperation to meet that development. A proposal to introduce burden distribution in order to receive refugees between the EU's member states is already on the EU's negotiating table. The different models being discussed are based, for example, on the size of countries' population, their GNP and other economic and social indicators. Norway comes off lucky on most such indicators. Norwegian participation in and responsibility for the migration issue is not set to diminish during the years to come. If the EU follows the same direction in this area as in other fields where serious crises have arisen, Norway will be confronted with major challenges. Because the EU countries share sovereignty, they also share responsibility. For Norway, it may be difficult to share responsibility for the joint effort in the field of migration without taking part in the supranational cooperation. On 18 March 2016, the EU countries agreed with Turkey to handle the flow of refugees. In return, among other things, Turkey will enjoy more lenient visa requirements for inward travel to the Schengen countries, including Norway.

CHAPTER 12

Part of, But Not a Member – or Vice Versa

Official Norwegian information has it that the EEA Agreement works just as well as EU membership for Norwegian companies, and the only thing Norway is missing out on is participating in the political fora. That is no longer the case. When times are good, the EEA is enough. When times get harder, it may prove inadequate.

These days Norway is as near as dammit part of the EU, just not a member. The whole of Norwegian society is intensely Europeanized save for farming. That much was established by the Norwegian Europe Review for the government-appointed Sejersted Committee.

The Norwegian economy is unarguably benefiting from income from the petroleum sector – income we have managed with exceptional acumen. Norway's economic conditions, which are entirely different from our neighbours', are down to our great oil wealth.

Norway's economy, however, consists of much more than petroleum products and associated service sectors. Norway has world-leading industrial players in aluminium, fertilizer and iron silicide. More recently, new sectors such as design, fashion and digital services have also developed. Since 1994, all governments have claimed that the EEA Agreement gives Norwegian business equal rights and the same market access to the EU's Single Market as all the EU countries. That is not correct. Since the start of the Single Market, trade between the EU countries has increased more than between the EU and Norway, as the Europe Review ascertains. The same applies to the scope of foreign investments. The EU countries have invested more with one another than in Norway. The Europe Review indicates that this is due to the difference between EEA and membership. In other words, Norwegian trade and economy might actually have fared better if Norway had been fully integrated in the whole EU cooperation.

One reason is that the EEA is not the same as the EU Customs Union. That is to say, Norway and the EU countries have different tariff rates on goods imported from countries outside the EU. In addition, Norway does not participate in the EU's cooperation on VAT, thereby exempting trade in goods and services from paying VAT, meaning that companies in an EU country set to trade with Norway must also introduce completely different accounting and customs clearance routines. This complicates two-way commerce and imposes extra work and expense on Norwegian exporters and importers. Top Norwegian clothing designers like Moods of Norway and by TiMo have set up their own companies in Sweden because redistribution, sales and payment are simpler inside the EU. They are not the only ones. A Swedish survey said Norway was more difficult to trade with than China. Online trading with other EU countries takes place on completely different terms than among the EU countries. Whereas all the EU countries have joint customs and VAT, Norwegian online customers are exempt from VAT right up to NOK 500. That is a boon for Norwegian consumers but a major drawback for Norwegian companies.

Following the merger with the German classification society Germanischer Lloyd, Det Norske Veritas (DNVGL) relocated its previous core operation, the classification of vessels, from Norway to Germany. One of the reasons is that the EU regulations governing classification societies do not become legally enforceable in Norway till 12-24 months after the EU countries. DNVGL's customers cannot wait for that.

It took five years from the time EU climate and energy legislation was proposed in 2007 until it was integrated in Norwegian law in 2012. In 2009 the British had already introduced one of the directives to increase the proportion of renewable energy by 2020. The British were able to offer competitive framework conditions for offshore wind – something Statoil and Statkraft launched into. Instead of the companies developing the technology in Norway, they took advantage of the EU's Single Market to invest in the extensive windpark off Sheringham Shoal off the east coast of England.

In Norway, the Stoltenberg government initially wished to keep the EU's renewable directive out of the EEA Agreement. When the government understood that it had no choice in the matter, it spent two years negotiating with the Commission as to how much new renewable power Norway should contribute. Although Norway already had the largest proportion of renewable energy of all the EU countries – over 60 percent of its total energy consumption – the EU felt that Norway had to engage in the EU's efforts to cut costs and create economies of scale. It was not until 2012, five and a half years after the Commission announced its commitment to renewable energy, that the government managed to agree on a Swedish-Norwegian certificate market for electricity. By that time, Statoil and Statkraft had been established in Great Britain since the start of 2009. They are now building one of Europe's largest offshore windparks, with 88 wind turbines, each of which will generate 3.6 MW electricity. It will supply 220,000 British homes with clean energy.

In 2002 the USA introduced an import embargo on steel owing to overproduction. The world's steel exporters then turned to the EU. The EU introduced protection measures to avoid destabilizing the European steel market. The Commission saw no reason to treat Norway any differently to other non-EU countries, despite trade in steel having its own protocol in the EEA Agreement. Three Norwegian companies were affected: Fundia and Rautaruukki in Mo i Rana and Corus in Bergen. Together they employ some 1,000 people, with total exports to the EU of NOK 1.3 billion in 2002, approx. 144.5 million euros.

Writing in *Aftenposten*, Ola Storeng commented that in this context the EEA Agreement was not worth the paper it is written on.[1]

These examples may explain why the impact of participating in the EU's Single Market has not been as great for Norway as for EU countries. The EEA Agreement has been adequate in good times, and particularly when the petroleum sector is the locomotive driving the economy. The situation can change quickly if Norway becomes more dependent on mainland commerce having to have framework conditions and market access equal to those of its competitors in the EU. As far back as 1994 many thought that even if the EEA Agreement looked after Norway's most important interests, it was inadequate. That has now become even clearer. As a result of a change of pace in the EU countries' form of cooperation, the business community's needs are no longer being met.

---

[1] O. Storeng, "Oljefondet stemte nei til Hellas-avtalen", *Aftenposten*, 18 May 2008.

Brexit: A solution for Norway? or vice versa?

On 24 January 2013, David Cameron announced that Great Britain would be renegotiating its EU membership. Then, if re-elected in 2015, he would organize a referendum, by the end of 2017, on whether Great Britain should leave or remain a member of the EU. Cameron's Conservative Party was coming under intense pressure from the anti-EU party UKIP (United Kingdom Independence Party), which was increasingly poaching voters from the Tory Party. UKIP won 27.5 percent[2] of the vote in the European Parliament elections of May 2014. Cameron therefore took the initiative of renegotiating British membership of the EU in areas such as social policy, employment and the environment. Here the prime minister thought that EU cooperation had gone too far.

Firstly, Cameron was sceptical of workers from Central and Eastern Europe 'stealing' jobs from Britons because they would accept, for Britons, unacceptably low wages. Secondly, Cameron wanted to see an end to "benefit shopping", and he also wanted to reduce benefit entitlements for job-seekers and employees from the new member states of Central and Eastern Europe. This problem received a great deal of publicity in Norway. The question hinged on whether a Pole paying tax and contributing to the Norwegian social security system should have the right to an equal level of sick pay and unemployment benefits when he goes back to Poland as others still living in Norway. This is the issue of cross-border social benefits. In addition, Great Britain has long argued against directives harmonizing working time provisions in the EU. Cameron, along with eminent politicians in the European Parliament, advocated adjusting the level of benefit payments according to the price level in the worker's country of origin. In the environmental field, the British wished to be exempted from a series of EU regulations like requirements to reduce air pollution, i.e. NO_x emissions. NO_x emissions are the source of acid precipitation that falls in Norway and destroys natural resources and air quality. Nor, according to Cameron, did directives to protect birds and other animals have any place in the EU conversation.

---

[2]   A. Hunt, "Vote 2014 at-a-Glance: The Big Winners Were UKIP", *BBC News*, 28 May 2014.

None of these proposals was put forward by accident. They are areas from the periphery of EU cooperation, where national and European legislation often come into conflict. They are also areas which take right-wing populist parties' views seriously. It is worth noting that Cameron did not ask for any derogations from the EU's "four freedoms": the free movement of labour and goods, people, services and capital over borders. Cameron, unlike his successor, was still in favour of Great Britain remaining in the EU's Single Market.

The British people voted to leave the EU on 23 June 2016. In March 2017 Prime Minister Theresa May invoked Article 50 of the Treaty on European Union, which set in motion Britain's withdrawal. The negotiations are proving tough because the other EU countries are none too inclined to give the British permanent derogations in areas they themselves find challenging. Giving in to British demands could run the risk of a domino effect that ends with the EU cooperation gradually breaking up – because if a country is granted dispensation from unpopular, but important, regulations, it can soon have a knock-on effect on others. On the other hand, there are many EU countries that are fed up of Great Britain holding up forms of cooperation which other states regard as necessary. A financial transaction tax, the so-called Tobin tax, is one such example. While France and Germany wish to introduce tax on trade in financial services to help finance development assistance or other good causes, the British see the Tobin tax as an assault on London's most important export article: financial services.

For Norway, the UK's negotiations with the EU will prove interesting. One option that would enable Britain's participation in the EU's Single Market is to join EFTA and thus retain membership of the EEA. The large democratic deficit and free movement of people will be key obstacles, precisely because of an apparent lack of sovereignty and resistance to labour immigration, which were stigmatized by the Leave campaign. However, with the growing fear of immigration in other major countries like France, the Netherlands, Germany and Sweden, Mrs May could find an audience sympathetic to tightening the principle of free movement of people. In fact, some countries have already pointed out that while the EU began with free movement of labour, it was later adapted to permit the free movement of people with no affiliation in the country they settle in. (Although Leave voters had fewer concerns about students and retirees than with active job-seekers.) Even EU protagonists, such as MEP Guy Verhofstadt, have argued for adjusting cross-border levels of social benefits.

As a non-EU member of the EEA, Great Britain will have to adhere to and respect the EFTA Court. This court is regarded as an independent European Court, although it bases its rulings on the Lisbon Treaty and EEA Agreement. However, a key difference is that its rulings are not legally binding to the same extent as the EU Court of Justice, as it has advisory status only. It cannot issue fines to economic actors, except in competition law. The EFTA states abide by its judgments voluntarily, in order to safeguard the legal homogeneity of the EEA Agreement. Furthermore, the EEA is not a customs union, meaning that the UK can conclude trade agreements of its own with third countries. As a member of the Single Market, the British would be able to make the case for having their own commissioner in order to be able to play a greater part in the EU's decision-shaping process. This could soften the brutality of becoming a "decision-taker", as the UK would be obliged to integrate large chunks of the EU acquis on a continual basis. This would, in fact, be in line with the spirit of the original concept of the EEA. Broader participation in the EU's decision-making process by the EFTA countries was indeed an essential aspect when Commission President Jacques Delors proposed the EEA in January 1989. However, at that time there was little political acceptance for the concept of a multi-speed Europe, as the case is today.

Another key aspect of the EEA option is that EFTA states do not pay anything into the EU budget towards the running of the EU institutions, other than specific programmes in which they take part, like the Horizon 2020 R&D programme, Culture etc. As an EEA EFTA state, the UK would have to pay a financial contribution directly to the Central and Eastern European countries that acceded post-2004 in order to contribute to European social and economic cohesion. The amount is based on bilateral negotiations and the money goes straight to the recipient countries' administrations, not via the EU institutions. Any EEA solution for the UK would have to be extended to cover market access in agriculture and fishery. From this angle, an EEA solution may emerge to be a relevant compromise when the British come to negotiate a new agreement that safeguards their participation in the Single Market while retaining sovereignty over trade policy and financial contributions. As is the case for Norway, the EEA option might turn out to be a national compromise for Britons: safeguarding economic interests at the cost of democratic participation; unloved by Brexiteers and Remainers alike, but not enough to embark on another painful and risky referendum. The down side, for both Norway and the UK, is that British EEA membership would cement the EEA as a viable long-term alternative for hesitant Europeans, making it more difficult to build the case for full membership.

Epilogue

Courageous Enough to Take on Europe?

The characteristic feature of Norway's approach to Europe and European cooperation has been the role of the straggler. We strung out our resistance to the Marshall Plan for as long as possible. We were having none of that Scandinavian and Nordic legally binding cooperation, and we ignored the European Coal and Steel Union. The list is as long as your arm.

In all these instances, the Norwegians have arrived after the event nevertheless, usually to negotiate special treatment. Often, the rationale behind our reluctance was that Norway has been a small, poor and vulnerable economy on the fringes of Europe, with industry and agriculture unable to compete with her neighbours. The upshot today is that Norway has fared extremely well despite all this scepticism towards international cooperation – better than most, in fact. Norway is a rich and prosperous country which the UN has chosen as the world's best country to live in. Today Europe sees a completely different Norway, which is both rich in resources and adaptable. Norway is the world's 23rd largest economy but ranks 118th in terms of population. We have fared better than others, which might suggest that the path we have taken was the right one. The reality, however, is that if things have gone so well, it is not because we were latecomers or out of the loop, but because we made it at the eleventh hour. Cooperation has benefited the Norwegians.

Norway has the world's largest offshore petroleum sector, the world's leading fish-farming industry, and power-intensive industries like aluminium, fertilizer and iron silicide. All these industries are offensive, competitive and adaptable, and all meet the conditions for taking part in the change-over to the low-carbon society. Norway is in a world-class category when it comes to arms sales. Even the Norwegian food industry, one of the counterforces in Norwegian internationalization down through the ages, has been internationalized. In 2012, 67 percent of Orkla Foods' revenue came from sales outside of Norway.[1] The low-key opening of the farmers' market in Mathallen, the Oslo Food Court built in 2012, attests to the great potential for niche products like Norwegian lamb, ham and alcohol. Norwegian cheese is already an international brand product.

Many will wonder whether this success is due precisely to our having been outside the EU. The answer, which also emerges from the Norwegian Europe Review, is that we actually *have* joined in. Not just that, but the Norwegian population are macro-consumers of the new European market in practice. We trade with, work, study and retire more in other countries in Europe than most EU countries themselves. In Norway, we exploit and benefit from opportunities which other countries have proposed, negotiated and implemented.

Norwegians have every possible reason to be proud of the society that has been built. However, we should also acknowledge that our social model is largely a result of binding cooperation with the countries around us. The time ought to be ripe to dare to be more open to taking part in the constant array of new initiatives that await us.

Norway, in other words, can no longer be the country that always hides away under the table or sits quiet as a mouse waiting for others to agree, as Knut Frydenlund described it.

Europe is in the process of taking fresh and altogether crucial steps to solve common problems. Commission President Jean-Claude Juncker's State of the Union in September 2017, followed by President Macron's Sorbonne speech, bear witness to an EU that is preparing to tackle a range of new policy areas in the field of defence, education, intelligence sharing, digital market, harmonization of taxation and new climate border taxation. The EU's new forms of cooperation on finance, energy, trade and migration testify to the fact that the EU is in the process of changing form and function. The new forms of cooperation are clearly putting the EEA to the test. These are new forms which the agreement has difficulty assimilating, because it is not sufficiently dynamic. Norway is going to find it more difficult to gain sympathy

---

[1]   Åge Korsvoll, President & CEO, Fourth quarter results 2012, 7 February 2013, Orkla.

for special and differential treatment in an increasingly large and more supranational EU. French President Emmanuel Macron's vision of a multi-speed EU can open the way for pragmatic new solutions where Norwegian interests can prevail, as for example in agriculture. Therefore, Norway's relationship with Europe is at a new crossroads. It is precisely because Norway has come as far as she has today, because she is so integrated, and because she is politically and economically strong compared to previously that Norwegians ought to be well placed to take part fully and exercise their influence on the vast changes taking place. That will benefit ourselves as well as the continent we are part of.

We can only hope that the generations that have followed since 1972 and 1994 will overcome their predecessors' fear of a new EU debate. If not, we run the risk of the next generation of young Norwegians who reap the benefits of our neighbours' initiatives being asked: Is Norway part of Europe?

Appendix

A Guide to Successful EU Lobbying

Norway's non-membership is a contributory factor in making many people feel awkward about taking on EU work. For the vast majority, the EU comes across as large and unwieldy. Those actively involved in dealings with the EU institutions often experience the opposite, that staff at the EU's bodies are open, approachable and amenable to being contacted. If you are going to work with the EU, however, you have to systematize your work. The chapter begins with what should be the point of departure for EU work: understanding the dynamics between the EU's institutions and establishing your level of ambition clearly. This is followed by a procedural method for lobbying work that I have developed over the twenty years I have been working in Brussels. Finally comes a model example to follow: the Erika case.

What Norway wants – about Norwegian navel-gazing and Finnish finesse

At a big maritime conference in Brussels some years ago a state secretary from the Norwegian Ministry of Trade and Industry gave a speech on framework conditions for shipping. Over the course of the 15 minute-long, intervention the state secretary used the word "Norway" 47 times: "Norway is the fifth-largest shipping nation in the world, Norway is the third-largest exporter of natural gas, Norway is the fourth-largest exporter of oil, Norway has the largest fish-farming industry in the world". Carrying on in that vein, it soon became rather embarrassing when people in the auditorium started to look at one another with raised eyebrows. In comparison, the following speech given by the British state secretary, mentioned Great Britain 11 times and the EU 27 times. A European conference wants to identify European solutions. The conferees may well enjoy listening to Norwegian experiences, but if it turns into a one-sided enumeration of national merits, people will fall by the wayside because it seems like out-and-out bragging. At another large maritime conference, European Maritime Day, the Norwegian state secretary also chose to talk about Norwegian Arctic policy, even though it was completely peripheral to the keynote conference topic. The reason was that the government had resolved to promote Norway's interests in the Arctic in any arena it got the chance. The address was received with astonishment.

Sweden, too, initially suffered from the exaggerated use of references to the way they themselves had solved problematic issues, often followed by a recommendation that the EU should introduce the same solution in the other member states. This went down very badly, especially in Southern Europe, where conditions are often vastly different. Part of the nub of EU cooperation is that countries sit down together and negotiate their way to common solutions to common problems. Furthermore, there are few countries that appreciate having textbook answers tossed onto the negotiating table. Coming to Brussels to showcase one's own solutions is both naive and counterproductive. The Swedish EU handbook for Swedish delegates to EU meetings also said that the most important thing was to identify Swedish interests. This is a useful starting point, but it must not blind delegates to the other countries' perspectives. Rather, the key to influence lies in one's ability to see things from other countries' perspectives. Finland has always been much better at this. Early on, the Finnish guide to EU work describes the first priority as being to identify which solutions are best from a holistic European perspective. The point of the EU cooperation, it says, is to devise common solutions to solve common problems. The Finnish manual points out the need to identify how Finnish interests can be dovetailed into possible European solutions. The Finns do not compromise on their own interests by any means, therefore, but the way they arrive at their negotiating position through reasoning makes their contributions interesting listening, and gives them greater influence over the debate and the outcome. In Brussels, the Finns, together with the Britons and the Germans, are considered top of the class at defending their interests and promoting constructive compromises. Finns are sought-after employees in the EU institutions. There are currently 518 Finns working at the Commission (the population of Finland is 5.2 million), while there are 520 Swedes (of Sweden's 9.2 million inhabitants) and 388 Danes (of Denmark's 5.5 million inhabitants). More than half of these work in managerial positions, from section heads right up to director-general and commissioner, giving representatives of our neighbours a considerable advantage.[2] They gain access to decision-makers more easily, enter into dialogue on matters of European policy at an early stage and can convey views to the right person at the right time. The Swedish EU Embassy, or Swedish Permanent Representation, as it is called in the language of the EU, has a special directory with the names and "points of single contact" of Swedes working in all the EU institutions. This is a new tool for Swedish administrators and lobbyists wishing to access information or discuss political problems with hundreds of their compatriots around the place in all the decision-making bodies. By way of comparison Norway has 46 national experts, meaning casework advisers in practice, at the European Commission.[3] None of them holds positions of appreciable political influence. Norwegian national experts can hold strategic posts nonetheless. For instance, the delegate from the Ministry of Health and Social Affairs was one of six executive officers at the Commission for the highly controversial Services Directive. The Norwegians are generally very helpful and willing to turn up to meetings and lectures when asked.

The EU's key institutions

Besides the European Commission the EU's most important institutions are the Council of Ministers, the European Council (the summit meeting that was institutionalized) and the European Parliament. (Many people use the terms "EU Commission" and "EU Parliament". These are not wrong, but in the Maastricht Treaty these institutions were given the names "European Commission" and "European Parliament".)

The Commission is responsible for drafting proposals for new legislation, and in 1980 and the early 1990s the Commission was certainly the most important of the EU institutions. But after the European

---

[2]   European Commission, staff figures, Brussels, http://ec.europa.eu/civil_service/about/figures/index_en.htm.

[3]   EFTA National Experts, EFTA Secretariat, http://ec.europa.eu/civil_service/about/figures/index_en.htm.

Parliament had its terms of reference extended and now has more or less the same role as the EU's member states, the Commission's role has changed considerably. These days the Commission is much more responsive to the political direction which the Parliament and the Council of Ministers wish to pursue. The problem is that the Parliament and the Council are often like cat and dog. While the EU's General Affairs Council, which consists of representatives of the EU countries' governments, is concerned with keeping the status quo, i.e. changing existing regulations in the home countries as little as possible, the Parliament is altogether different. There the level of ambition is much higher.

The Parliament: Europe's most important political arena

Generally speaking, the European Parliament wishes to replace national regulations with a new, joint regulatory framework. It is one of the few places that EU policy is discussed and negotiated largely on the basis of what is best for Europe collectively, not just for national interests. The European Parliament has evolved into Europe's most important political arena.

The new EU treaties negotiated in Maastricht in 1991, Amsterdam in 1995 and Nice in 2001, all shared one important feature: they gave the European Parliament formal legal authority, which is to say more influence and power. The Parliament has gradually acquired the legal right to adopt EU legislation on an equal footing with the member states on the EU's Council of Ministers. It was the French President François Mitterrand who, during the Maastricht negotiations in 1989, insisted that whenever countries in the EU lost the chance to issue a veto, the loss of national sovereignty would be offset by granting co-determination in the European Parliament. That is to say that the European Parliament must endorse whatever is determined in all areas where decisions are taken on the EU's Council of Ministers with a two-thirds majority. In 1992 this co-determination procedure applied only to the most important parts of the Single Market. Today the Parliament has the right of co-determination in all areas save for social and welfare policy, defence and foreign policy, and tax. If the EU wishes to make a decision in these three areas, all countries must be in agreement – which in practice means each country having a right of veto. And that is how it was until the Single European Act was adopted in 1986, which contributed to the EU cooperation being mostly paralyzed until then. In 20 years, from 1979 to 1999, the European Parliament went from virtually being a chit-chat club for appointed representatives from national popular assemblies with no real power to a directly popularly elected legislative assembly with the right to adopt EU laws like the member states' own governments. This radical change added impetus to the Parliament's political work and activities. It became ever more important for the Parliament to make its mark and promote its own political solutions to the Commission and the Council of Ministers. This development first culminated in 2001, when the Parliament refused to accept the EU budget, thereby forcing Commission President Jacques Santer to resign. A more recent example is when, during the parliamentary elections of May 2014, the European Parliament promoted its own candidates for the office of President of the Commission. The Lisbon Treaty does open the way for this, admittedly, but in slightly unclear terms, because this possibility was the subject of intense negotiations when the treaty was drawn up. After a long tug-of-war the EU's heads of state on the European Council, which had hitherto been responsible for appointing the President of the European Commission, chose to accept the Parliament's candidate. Luxembourg's ex-Prime Minister, Jean Claude Juncker, is therefore the first popularly elected President of the European Commission.

Today the Parliament has consolidated its position in negotiations with the member states and the Commission on the contents of all EU legislation. It was the European Parliament, for example, that arranged to have the adoption of the regulations regarding restrictions on the use of chemicals, REACH,[4] tightened up after the member states attempted to dilute the Commission's proposal. The member states thought the regulations would diminish the industry's competitiveness and result in lower economic growth with increased unemployment – arguments which are perfectly normal when the Commission proposes stringent environmental requirements. Today REACH has become a global

---

[4]   REACH stands for Registration, Evaluation, Authorization and Restriction of Chemicals, and is considered to be the world's strictest legislation governing the use of chemicals.

standard to which most industrialized countries in the world adhere. The reason is that the EU regulations place responsibility firmly with those importing products made outside the EU. If importers do not comply with the regulations, they can lose the right to import the good or be fined. Because the EU is the world's largest market, big companies have introduced the EU requirements for products that are sold all over the world in order to save time and energy adjusting to different requirements in different markets. In this way the EU contributes to setting standards not just in Europe but also in the rest of the world.

There are many examples. Japanese and Korean car manufacturers currently sell cars that satisfy the EU's NOx emission requirements in Asia and Latin America, even though these countries do not have equally strict regulations as the EU. Using the Services Directive, the Parliament restricted the possibilities of working in other EU countries on the same pay conditions as in the country of origin. The European Parliament also showed its teeth in the work on the EU's energy and climate package, where the Parliament pressured member states into accepting the Commission's proposal for a 20 percent reduction in greenhouse gas emissions by 2020. The Parliament also played an important role when the EU's climate target for 2030 had to be fixed by putting pressure on the member states ahead of the summit in October 2014, when the EU's heads of state advocated cutting greenhouse gas emissions by 40 percent by 2030. The European Parliament's powerful support for EU Telecom Commissioner Neelie Kroes' revolutionary proposal to remove the roaming charges for mobile phones within the EU and reduce the cost of surfing the Internet was also crucial. It is highly unlikely that this proposal would have been adopted if it had been up to the member states alone, since national telecom companies traditionally enjoy a strong position in the vast majority of EU countries.

The European Parliament offers greater opportunities to promote Norwegian political interests than any other EU institution. Sigbjørn Johnsen, Norway's Minister of Finance in the Stoltenberg II government, made diligent use of the Parliament when he was trying to win colleagues over to the need for a Norwegian derogation from the EU's Deposit Guarantee Scheme Directive in banks. A government guarantee for bank deposits ensures that customers get their savings back if the banks go to the wall. Lately, banks have been using the profits from their customary banking, i.e. saving and lending, to make investments on the international finance market. The dividing line between traditional savings banks, financial institutions and insurance companies has been obliterated, which may lead to small-time savers' money being jeopardized if the banks go under. The financial crisis of 2008 was an example of this. While the government guarantees deposits of up to NOK 2 million in Norway, the EU countries settled on harmonizing the 100,000 euro government guarantee, the equivalent of about NOK 930,000. There were two reasons why the EU cooperation agreed to harmonize 100,000 euro. Firstly, the occurrence of the financial crisis in 2008 showed that people were moving their savings to countries with higher deposit guarantees. For example, many Icelanders moved their money to Norway. In times of crisis it is important to have calm in the market and avoid people moving money from bank to bank. Secondly, the size of the deposit guarantee is a form of support for the bank. The greater the guarantee, the more risk the banks can take because they know the government will cover a larger amount if anything goes wrong.

After extensive contact with the European Parliament's rapporteur for the bank deposit guarantee scheme on the Internal Market Committee, Johnsen eventually gained support for a draft amendment that could give Norway a four-year transition period. The work put into this matter was massive. The Norwegian Ministry of Foreign Affairs instructed all embassies in the EU countries to assign top priority to the matter, but it was the work interfacing with the European Parliament that paid off. Johnsen managed to get the parliamentary rapporteur to table a draft amendment of his own that had been tailor-made to secure Norway a four-year transition period in the original directive. In Norway, this was viewed as a breakthrough for the government's wishes, though Norway will have to adjust the guarantee downwards for Norwegian banks in 2018.

Other Norwegian players who used the Parliament as an arena to achieve a breakthrough for their interests in exploiting and protecting resources in the Arctic include the North Norway Office in particular.

The European Commission

The European Commission continues to be an important institution. In 1992, when Norway negotiated the EEA Agreement, the Commission was in the driving seat and was the institution that set the EU's political agenda. That is no longer the case. The Commission is still responsible for drawing up new legislation and is therefore important to keep abreast of, while its role has developed considerably over the past 20 years. Today the Commission acts more as a broker between the member states' Council of Ministers and the popularly elected representatives at the European Parliament. The story of the Erika case towards the end of the chapter gives an impression of the role the Commission can play. The Commission must also see to it that laws are properly implemented and enforced, as EFTA's surveillance authority, ESA, does for Norway's part. But the Commission's task of developing new policies and new regulations is what is most important, and ESA does not have this function.

The EU's General Affairs Council

The council of the member states – be it the Council of Ministers, the summit or the European Council – still formally constitutes the most important institutions in the EU's decision-making machinery. These should not be confused with the Council of Europe, where MPs from 47 countries throughout Europe sit and Torbjørn Jagland is Secretary-General. The Council of Ministers' working parties, particularly COREPER (the Permanent Representatives' Committee), where the ambassadors prepare cases for their ministers or heads of state, are important. This is where the EU's member states can negotiate between various specialist fields. For instance, Lithuania had to cede a good deal in the Service Directive because the country had to give up the requirement that Lithuanian workers could work in other EU countries for domestic rates of pay.

In another parallel case about telecommunications the other ambassadors remembered that Lithuania "took one for the team" in connection with the Service Directive and displayed extra patience and respect for the country's interests. Norway's EU ambassador from 2001-2005,

Bjørn Grydeland, used the expression "IOUs"; that is, every EU country knows exactly what each country has given and received in negotiations. Whenever a country has to be particularly accommodating in one area, it will be given an 'IOU' that can be redeemed in negotiations in another field. On this basis, some countries can be granted permanent derogations or in other cases generous transitional arrangements.

Three levels of ambition for EU work

Systematic work on EU policy is conditional on first having a clear idea about one's level of ambition. Not everyone wishes to change EU policies. Many are content to keep track of what is happening in order to prepare for new political initiatives and regulations. So, the first level of ambition for EU work is to keep abreast of developments. The Commission's work programme is the key here. Every year the Commission publishes an overview of all legislative proposals with specific lists of the legislative proposals already lined up for consideration by the Council and the Parliament, or new proposals they intend to produce. Green papers are often the term given to a notice from the Commission merely establishing facts and describing the situation in a particular policy field. A number of conferences are always organized, both in Brussels and usually in the country holding the travelling or itinerant presidency. Dedicated websites with consultations are created, which also provide access to comments and input from other players. A white paper is a report outlining what the Commission has decided the new policy proposal will look like. It often contains proposals for a specific wording to be presented to the Council and the Parliament, as well as the committees for the social partners and the regions.

The next level of ambition is to get involved in the work of developing the legislation. In "Brusselsese" it is called 'surgical lobbying'. The point here is to produce concrete draft amendments for key people in the EU's decision-making bodies: the Commission, the European Parliament or the Council of Ministers. This is where the expression "it's important to make friends before you need them" comes in. Whether it is a matter of energy policy or waste policy, there are generally no more than a dozen people responsible for the matter in the whole of the EU system. Good personal relations with these people are an advantage, but not a prerequisite. The point is to know who they are and to be able to call on them whenever a problem or possibility arises. Often, for example, the Commission's officer in charge will work closely together with the European Parliament's advisers on concrete proposals. It is entirely possible to arrange meetings and explain complex, convoluted remits to the right individuals in all three decision-making bodies. However, it is a clear condition that both advisers and the company representative wishing to contact the person in charge of the case at the EU institutions have registered with the European Parliament's 'transparency register', or the lobby register, as it is often referred to in the Norwegian media. In meetings with representatives from the EU institutions it is important to put forward arguments that not merely serve one's own interests but also have an overall European perspective. Written representations, in the form of a draft legislative text or a policy paper, are often desirable as these can also be posted on the website or recorded in the MPs' log of representations received. In this situation, it is also essential for several players, preferably from different walks of life, band together and agree on a joint political message. Few people, if any, accomplish anything in Brussels singlehandedly. The broader the coalitions and alliances between European players for industry segments, the environment and trade unions, the greater the potential for success.

The third and last level of ambition is to get into a situation where one becomes a supplier of terms for EU policy development. In Brussels, this is called a 'trusted stakeholder', i.e. a player who commands so much knowledge, about both policy and specialist content, that he or she is invited as a contributor when the Commission's experts investigate how the new policy is going to look. That may sound odd, but it is precisely like the roles the Norwegian Shipowners' Association and the Federation of Agricultural Co-operatives play in developing Norwegian maritime and farming policy. These are organizations that have been monitoring Norwegian policy development in their fields for a long time, who have great resources and possess a great deal of specialist competence. How can a Norwegian player achieve such a position at EU level? What follows here are my four commandments and excellent examples of Norwegian lobby work.

The first commandment: Think European!

If you are going to succeed at lobbying the EU institutions, it is important to position your message in a European setting. It's called "thinking European", and contrasts with thinking nationally or even more narrowly: focusing just on your own goals. The benefits of framing one's interests in a greater perspective are no great secret, and precisely what the Norwegian special-interest organizations do when working with the *Storting* and Norwegian civil service. The political scientist Hilmar Rommetvedt used the expression *allmenngjøringstesen* (the "thesis of universal applicability") – that which places individual interests in a broader context. In this instance, the point is to frame one's interests in a European perspective – a kind of Europeanized universal applicability.

For some reason, this procedure has been relegated to oblivion for many people. When Norwegians arrive in Brussels, far too often they feel a strong need to accentuate Norwegian conditions and compare themselves with other countries, as when the state secretary from the Ministry of Trade and Industry mentioned "Norway" 47 times in 15 minutes.

A Norwegian representative who has no political allies to rely on for support must be much cleverer than his or her colleagues in the EU countries at devising good solutions for Europe as a whole. Norwegian input is measured on its merits, not on the weight of meat on the scales. There is no meat on the scales for Norway's part.

The mistake most people make is to ask: "What does the EU do in the field we are working on?", only to then run through lists of the Commission's work programme, directives and regulations in the pipeline, or already adopted and due to go into the EEA Agreement. Then it all rapidly goes haywire. It is useful to have an overview of existing activities, but for anyone who aspires to change EU policy, it is better to turn the problem around: What are our objectives and how can the EU contribute to achieving these? You can then put your political goals first, get a head-start over the EU's work and contribute to thinking outside the box. The likelihood of other EU countries struggling with the same problem is great, and this can act as a pointer to political allies.

Second commandment: Use the right arena!

The EU institutions have different tasks and status. Working intimately with such institutions must reflect this.

The European Commission, as mentioned, still has responsibility for drawing up new legislation and is therefore important to keep abreast of. Lobbying work targeted at the Commission should be based on technical or fact-based arguments that will better enable the Commission to play the role of mediator between the Council and the European Parliament.

The EU's General Affairs Council represents the institutions populated by the EU's ministers and heads of state. Here the representatives of the EU member states negotiate, often on the basis of what is considered best for their member states, often with the aim of preserving the status quo. Work done at close quarters with the EU's General Affairs Council must therefore attach importance to the least possible transfer of competence from member states to the EU, identify and point out the advantages that national players can achieve, and spell out the financial consequences – or indeed, the advantages or economies to be gained. The Council of Ministers' working parties are important. Here the EU's member states negotiate between various specialist fields and think in both political, technical and budgetary terms, so that new laws will not have too great a financial impact. The rotating presidency sets the agenda and should thus be regarded as a prime target for anyone wishing to partake in EU policy development.

The European Parliament has developed into Europe's and Norway's most important political arena, both politically and legally. Since the European Parliament's point of departure is often Europe's collective interests and a desire for a common, European regulatory framework in several fields, EMPs are much more amenable to new ideas and methods. They have no regard for where the idea comes from or who is behind it. For Norway, therefore, the Parliament is absolutely the most important and best arena in which to conduct lobbying work, and our oasis when it comes to policies on Europe. This is the easiest place to source information and take part in policy development, so it is important to become acquainted with MEPs who have an appreciation of the matter and are willing to promote the message. The way to become a supplier of terms to the European Parliament is to identify how proposed measures can strengthen Europe's role globally and focus on the proposal's impact on creating added value and employment.

Also of possible benefit is the fact that EMPs are known for moving between the Brussels HQ, where party groups and committee meetings take place, and one-week plenary meetings in Strasbourg. This should please those of us in Norway greatly. When all 751 MEPs siege in Strasbourg, it provides a wealth of opportunities to touch bases with the MEPs or their assistants and advisers, either on the plane or train, at the hotel, or in the charming restaurant area of "Petite France".

Third commandment: Leave yourself plenty of time

You need a long-term perspective on EU work. Firstly, it generally takes one or two years to build up a network in Brussels, a network that should not only consist of representatives from the Commission and the Parliament but also other member states, NGOs and interested parties from industry. In the example from Bellona's work described in Chapter 5, it took five years from the time CCS technology was launched in Parliament until the directive and financing scheme were proposed by the Commission. Then it took a further two years to successfully negotiate the proposals and three years before they were implemented. An eight to ten years perspective of this kind may be necessary when working at close quarters with EU institutions, so the Norwegian system of replacing staff in the EU delegation every two to three years is not very constructive. Norwegian diplomats barely get to set up a network before they have to go back again. Language can also be an obstacle. Norwegian diplomats are often sent to Brussels without being able to speak French, which has traditionally been one of the main languages in the EU. All Swedish and Danish diplomats have to know French in order to work in their permanent representation, i.e. their embassies to the EU, in Brussels. If they cannot speak French, they are sent on a three-month language course, the bulk of which takes place in France.

Short diplomatic postings are a challenge for the EU countries too, but not to the same extent as for Norway: government delegates are not convened to the Council of Ministers' meetings – meetings which automatically furnish delegates from other countries with a network and knowledge. Many Norwegian companies and organizations have taken this on board. For example, Åse Erdal and Yaras Steinar Solheim from KS benefit greatly from having been in Brussels for two decades, and Norsk Hydro's Jan-Peter Jebsen has been back for a second term.

Fourth commandment: Forge alliances and network

The EU cooperation is a wide-ranging collaborative project. It is not one door or one mailbox. When I gave a talk to a large Norwegian aquafarming company, many people were up in arms about the EU's measures to regulate the price of salmon – in this case the introduction of a minimum price for Norwegian salmon. I asked what action they had taken to raise awareness of their cause in Brussels. Then someone from the back of the room yelled: "We sent them a letter explaining that jobs are at stake!" The problem is precisely that jobs are at stake in all countries where salmon production is competing with Norwegian production. Given that these countries' representatives hawk their case around the gamut of EU institutions to plead their cause, sending a letter in the post is very unconstructive.

Political sympathy can only be won in the Parliament if support from other players can be mobilized. No one achieves good results by acting alone in the European Parliament. Building alliances is altogether central, whether to obtain a consensus from trendsetting member states, industrial organizations or organizations representing civil society. Diplomacy and networking are therefore a central part of the work. Being present over time is altogether central in this context. The optimal lobbying strategy is to gather allies from industry, trade unions and NGOs, just as in Norway. The challenge is that it takes more time, resources and contacts to build such networks in Brussels than in Oslo. In Brussels, they reckon it takes about two to three years to build up a network of contacts and allies from business interests, NGOs and others. Such alliances are easier to achieve by focusing on finding common European solutions, and by showing enthusiasm for the EU project.

An example to emulate – the Erika case

There are many very able Norwegian senior officials who do a sterling and extremely important job of promoting Norwegian interests on the many different expert committees set up by the Commission. The most important include committees with representatives of all the EU and EEA countries engaged in food safety, the use of chemicals in industry or consumer rights and so on. What often characterizes Norwegian senior officials participating in these committees is that they are pro-Europe enthusiasts with a fine talent for making contact with colleagues in the EU member states. They are good at entering into alliances with others, and not least they make sure they win sympathy among the hierarchy in the directorate or ministry back home for the case they are working on. One of the foremost examples of success in promoting Norwegian shipping interests in the EU is the job done by Mr Leif Asbjørn Nygaard, ex-Director-General of the Ministry of Trade, Industry and Fisheries.

When the Maltese tanker M/S Erika was wrecked and went down off the coast of Brittany in December 1999, it set off alarm bells at the Commission's Directorate-General for Energy and Transport, DG TREN. 31,000 tonnes of crude oil escaped from the ship, spreading out along 400 km of French coastline and destroying the marine environment, including important business interests and the lovely tourist beaches. The incident triggered a political earthquake in France, and people expected the authorities to step in. The French President, Jacques Chirac, was due to take over the EU presidency six months later and wanted to show France that the EU could serve French interests. He therefore asked his Prime Minister, Lionel Jospin, to inform his colleagues on the European Council that France wished to negotiate an EU directive under the French presidency that would render such accidents impossible in future.

The Commission was all but ordered to initiate a full-scale project to form an overview of the quality and age of Europe's tanker fleet and make a study of the IMO's existing regulations. From the time of the accident on 12 December 1999 to 21 February the following year, the Commission prepared three comprehensive draft directives in the "Erika 1" package: (1) tightening of inspections of vessels in ports,

(2) increased responsibility for the classification societies and (3) accelerated phasing-out of single-hull ships.

Before the Commission's College of Commissioners was due to adopt the proposals for forwarding to the Council of Ministers and the Parliament, the Commission convened meetings with experts from all the EU and EFTA countries, as provided for by the EEA Agreement.

The first challenge for the Norwegians attending the Commission's expert meeting was the timing aspect. The invitation arrived barely two weeks before the meeting was due to take place. That left precious little time to obtain the views of relevant parties in Norway, like the Maritime Directorate, the Shipowners' Association, the Seafarers' Union and the Ministry of the Environment. There was even less time to obtain a politically clear-cut negotiating position at ministerial policy level. Here Norway's situation differs from that of the EU member states; for Norway, this meeting is the one time Norwegian experts are invited to take part in a meeting at the EU to discuss the contents of the directives. If the Norwegian expert is to be able to present the Norwegian negotiating position, a consultation round must be held. In this and many other instances, there was insufficient time for a consultation round. The other challenge for the Norwegian experts is the lack of a political mandate to take a stand on difficult political deliberations. In as much as the Commission's drafts of directives are often marked confidential, the administration is reluctant to circulate directive proposals until they have been finally approved by the Commission. Thus, many Norwegian experts keep their seats without a negotiating mandate and regard the meeting merely as an opportunity to keep up to date with developments in the EU, not as a forum for promoting Norwegian points of view.

Experts in the EU countries, on the other hand, are not expected to present any national view at this stage of the process; this is not expected until the proposal is presented to the Council of Ministers and the European Parliament. The expert has been invited on the basis of his own competence and hence does not represent national interests.

The meeting of experts at which the Commission presented the Erika package at the beginning of March 2000 was attended by Director-General Leif Asbjørn Nygaard together with experts from the Norwegian Maritime Directorate and the Ministry of the Environment. For Norwegian interests the thing of particular importance was the legislative proposal to decommission tankers with just one hull from European waters. The Commission had been pushing for an accelerated phase-out that would take far less time than existing legislation within the UN's maritime organization (IMO). The Norwegian tanker fleet was one of the most modern in the world, but few of the tanker vessels were double-hulled. Norway is one of the world's leading shipping nations and for the past hundred years has had one of the world's largest fleets. The skills of Norwegian mariners and shipping lines have provided invaluable insight into the way quality shipping can be operated, a fact from which the Norwegian Maritime Directorate and shipping politicians benefit. The Norwegian view of this matter was that it is not necessarily the number of hulls that is decisive for safety, but rather how the vessel is operated and maintained. The Norwegian fleet, as mentioned, had few vessels with a double hull, so that an EU order issued before the advent of the IMO would have proved costly for Norwegian shipping companies. The Norwegian chief negotiator was therefore ordered to garner support for the Norwegian point of view while the Commission's proposal was under discussion.

The meeting was opened by Georgette Lalis, the Greek Director for Maritime Transport at the Commission's Directorate-General for Energy and Transport, DG TREN. Since Greece is the EU's largest shipping nation, this post is generally occupied buy a Greek. After DG TREN's Unit Head, Wim De Ruiter, introduced the first proposal to tighten up port state controls, they went round the table in alphabetical order, this time starting from the back with the UK, going from one country to another until the round ended with Belgium. The discrepancies were sizable.

The British saw no need for new laws. What they needed was more resources to perform more frequent inspections of incoming vessels. They were supported by the Greeks, who owing to the low standard of their fleet, were rarely eager to have new and tighter rules. The French, by contrast, wanted the EU to step into the breach for other countries in the IMO and adopt a more stringent set of regulations for inspecting vessels putting in at ports in EU countries. The USA had done the same thing after the accident in Alaska with the Exxon Valdez in 1989, in which more than 1 million tonnes of crude oil caused massive damage to the marine environment, fauna and flora. So, there was no reason why the EU countries could not also spearhead the campaign for stricter regulations. The Netherlands and Germany supported the French proposal, but insisted on the EU trying to push through the same requirements in the IMO. And so they carried on round the table right until Belgium at the end had commented on the Commission's proposal. That was when Norway took the floor: "And now I have the pleasure of inviting our friends from the EFTA states to take the floor. Norway, would you like to start?" said Wim De Ruiter. Iceland and Liechtenstein have severely limited economies and rarely take part in the Commission's expert meetings unless they are about the safety of fishing vessels or the financial market.

Such situations put Norwegian experts to the test. Having to state one's views on a legislative proposal after all the countries have taken orderly turns to comment on, criticize and suggest changes is no easy matter. You usually get in a word or two right towards the end of the meeting, when people are worn out and impatient, because they would rather go home. The contribution by Norwegian experts is generally restricted to extending polite thanks for the invitation, stressing that this is a discussion Norway is following with great interest and saying that they would appreciate being invited to the next meeting. It was different at this meeting. Leif Asbjørn Nygaard was exceptionally well known in international shipping policy circles. He had taken part in numerous negotiations in other international fora like UNCTAD, the OECD and the IMO, and had even sat on the EU's Council of Ministers' working party during the "engagement period" – from the time Norway had completed negotiations on its EU membership agreement until the referendum on 28 November 1994. Not only did Nygaard know most of the experts around the table personally, he knew exactly what interests they were defending and what arguments they were using. Nygaard also spoke excellent negotiating English: short sentences, logical, with simple yet meaningful words that made it easy for the simultaneous translators behind the big glass windows to understand and convey to the other participants. Nygaard managed to capture the others' interest by building bridges between the trendsetting member states, the British on the one hand and the French on the other, and helped the Commission to find an acceptable compromise. In his succinct and readily comprehensible fashion, he explained how international shipping works and how important it is to give the regulations universal anchorage. The EU's objectives and role consisted of presenting a unified front in order to forge alliances that would make an impact on the International Maritime Organization (IMO), Nygaard stressed. The Commission expressed its gratitude for Nygaard's contribution. When the meeting reached its last and most important item on the agenda for Norway, the question of phasing out single-hull ships, Wim De Ruiter called on the Norwegian expert first. Taking the floor first was a great advantage, and Nygaard laid the foundation for the ongoing discussion, thereby helping to ensure that the Commission's proposal was toned down appreciably. That gave Norwegian shipping companies valuable extra time to phase out single-hull vessels from the EU/EEA countries' waters and deferred expensive investments. It was a masterclass in Norwegian involvement work at the EU.

EU involvement is a much greater challenge for Norway than for our colleagues in the EU countries because we have no representatives or staff at the EU's key institutions. Norwegians have to cultivate understanding and sympathy, earn recognition – call it sympathy or whatever – on the part of senior officials and politicians who are not from Norway. It requires exceptionally good professional insight combined with political intuition and good communication skills. In the EU cooperation, representatives from Norwegian authorities, civil society and the business community have common issues. They are in a boxing ring with their hands tied behind their backs. It takes particularly agile footwork and body feints to avoid being knocked down. The day Norway becomes a member, we will have Norwegians in top posts and will take over the Brits' and the Finns' positions as leading suppliers of terms and negotiators in the EU's decision-making machinery.

Index of Keywords

Chirac, Jacques 108, 219
Churchill, Winston 39, 40, 53, 58, 65, 98
Claes, Dag Harald 139, 142
Coca-Cola Company 72
Cockfield, Arthur 80
Coudenhove-Kalergi, Richard Nikolaus 33, 39
Council of Europe 53, 54, 63, 145, 212

D

Dalton, Hugh 29
Davies, Chris 154
Dawes, Charles 34
de Gaulle, Charles 64, 65, 76
Defence alliance with Great Britain 38
Delors, Jacques 35, 61, 81, 83, 84, 86, 87, 91, 93, 95, 97, 120, 187
Dimas, Stavros 154
DNV GL 194

E

E.ON 151, 180
EFTA's Surveillance Authority (ESA) 12, 138, 171, 173, 212, 162, 186, 188
Eden, Anthony 60
Edward VII, King of England 31
Einstein, Albert 33
Électricité de France (EDF) 151
Enger, Anne 101, 103, 115, 121

Erlander, Tage 43
European Consumer Organization (BEUC) 185
European Convention on Human Rights 49
European Court of Human Rights 53
European Movement 46, 51, 90, 101, 130, 186
Europautredningen (Norwegian Europe Review) 15, 55, 80, 89, 113, 114, 115, 117, 133-135, 139, 141, 193, 202

F

Financial crisis in 2008 164, 211
First World War 31, 32, 46, 76, 111
Five, Kaci Kullmann 86, 96
Food Court (*Mathallen*) in Oslo 202
French Revolution 41
Freud, Sigmund 33
Frisvold, Paal 36, 37, 52
Frontex 190
Frydenlund, Knut 15, 69, 85, 87, 202

G

Gambetta, Léon 21
Gas Market Directive 126, 128, 132, 133, 135, 139-142
Gazprom 177, 179, 180
General Electric 151

"Europe of Cultures"

Series Director: Léonce BEKEMANS

"*Europe of Cultures*" is a series of studies, monographs, stories, research projects, reports on conferences and debates devoted to the complexities and changing realities in European societies. It bridges the past with the future at the cross road of challenges and opportunities of the transformation of European societies. The management of changes in societies refers to the interconnection of various dimensions and levels of policy-making impacting on economic, social, political, democratic, communication, philosophical, artistic, religious as well as ethical traditions and behaviour. As an editorial project the series is structured along two interconnected and complementary sub-series: i.e. the "*(Europe of) Dialogues*" series and the "*(Europe of) Living Stories*".

- The sub-series "*(Europe of) Dialogues*" mainly deals with (cultural) diversities, identity and citizenship building in Europe as well as with the relevant multi-level governance and communication structures in the transformation of European societies. Europe is a laboratory for understanding this multi- and intercultural reality. The purpose is to contribute to a better understanding and communication of the changes taking place by looking at the European societies in general, and the specificities of different national, regional and local cultures and communities in a framework of dialogues. The series presents interdisciplinary and critical views of value-driven and policy-oriented reflections. Moreover, it offers new insights into understanding how to manage, value and communicate cultural diversity, identity and citizenship. It also wants to contribute to the development of new ways of "living together", in which cultures and communities are perceived as binding forces in creative society building.

- The sub-series "*(Europe of) Living Stories*" (the former "*Mémoires de l'Europe en devenir*", Director Gabriel Fragnière †) is devoted to inspiring narratives for a broad public with a view to contribute to a better understanding, communication and contextualisation of the newly emerging Europe. It mainly focusses on stories, memories and testimonies of persons, events, institutions and issues that have transformed mentalities, fostered European awareness and finally shaped Europe's future. These stories serve as important references and communication tools for future developments of Europe in the world. This collection wants to be open in its content, method and pedagogy faithful to Europe's role and reference in the globalising world.

Editorial Board

Raphaela Averkorn, *Jean Monnet Professor ad personam, University of Siegen*

Martyn Barrett, *Emeritus Professor of Psychology, University of Surrey*

Franco Bianchini, *Professor of Cultural Policy and Planning, Leeds Metropolitan University*

Victoria Martin De La Torre, *Press Officer Group of the Progressive Alliance of Socialists & Democrats in the European Parliament*

Luciano Morganti, *Professor, Free University Brussels*

Antonella Valmorbida, *Director, Association of Local Democracy*

Joke van der Leeuw-Roord, *founder and former Director of EUROCLIO – European Association of History Educators, The Hague*

Inés Verplancke, *Coordinator "Ryckevelde", European Center of Active Citizenship, Bruges*

Albin Wagener, *Professor, Faculty of Humanities, Université catholique de l'Ouest, Angers*

Published titles

www.peterlang.com